Almeda. March 3d 1869.

John, dear,

I intended writing to you Saturday, but
ma and Sabra were sick, Addie was from home and I
had company, so that my time was too fully occupied
for me to write. Ma was taken sick Thursday night-
and for two days was very, very sick. Since that she has
been gradually improving. She thought when I left this
morning she would be able to sit- up some today. Sabra
has been at her father's house sick nearly two weeks. She
is not confined to bed- but suffers most- of the time
with head ache. You know we must miss her very much.
Cordelia has been over several times and rendered some assistance.
Jimmie Morrow came by early last Wednesday morning
with his wagon lightly laden with pork. flour, butter &c.
going to Raleigh. He offered to take Addie as far as
Chapel Hill and she accepted the offer & was in & off in
a few minutes- They returned Saturday night after dark.
Addie left Nellie & family well. She spent one night at
Mr. Mickles. She has, as is always the case with her when she
returns after a trip from home; a great deal to tell of what she
heard. saw, said & did while she was gone. She visited Mr Wilson's
singing school and was more charmed with the children's singing
than any thing else. She says I must tell you little
Sallie Mallett is at St Mary's. An Illinois gentleman

The Schoolmaker

The Schoolmaker

SAWNEY WEBB
and the BELL BUCKLE STORY

by *Laurence McMillin*

The University of
North Carolina Press
Chapel Hill

Manufactured in the United States of America
ISBN 0–8078–1163–7
Library of Congress Catalog Card Number 72–144336

To my wife Marguerite
OUR *book*

Contents

Illustrations

Foreword

Bell Buckle, Tennessee, lies some fifty miles southeast of Nashville on the main line to Chattanooga, and in the autumn of 1929 the railroad was almost the only link between this tiny village and the outside world. It was possible to drive to and from Nashville, but the road was not very good and there were no buses. So those who would come there from distant places journeyed to either Nashville or Chattanooga, caught the Dixie Flyer and asked the conductor to make an unscheduled stop. On this particular autumn day, as for some forty years past, the train rumbled to a halt and a covey of young boys tumbled out of the cars, some jostling each other amid loud whoops as they greeted old friends, some silent and uncertain.

For the uncertain ones the village itself offered small reassurance. A cluster of country stores around the railroad plaza, a few unpaved streets, a church steeple in the distance; that was all. Even after trudging up the hill, the vista was no more prepossessing. The schoolyard, the mecca for all this journeying, covered only a few acres. In the center was a huge, wooden-framed cavern that looked like a barn for cows. Dotted around it were several one-room, clapboard buildings. The only sign of brick and mortar lay across a dusty playground. This, as it turned out, was the library; the books were much better housed than the boys.

The first impression for a city boy, and one to stay with me for a lifetime, was of a ghost town right out of those silent movies at the Alamo theater back home, a town that time and progress had forgot. The impression was confirmed daily. Mrs. Sturdevant's boarding house, where a dozen boys were mothered by this buxom widow, had a privy in the back, and the luxury of washing depended on the rainfall caught on the tin roof and drained into a cistern. Those little clapboard buildings, which proved to be classrooms, were heated with a pot-bellied stove; the Big Room, which took up most of the barn-like structures, had two.

You knew without anybody telling you that Bell Buckle had changed little since the Webb School moved there in 1886; neither had the school, for all that some of the older boys got to live in a regular dormitory beyond the schoolyard. And you didn't have to be there long before you knew that this ghost town had a real ghost. Dead these three years, Old Sawney Webb stalked the classrooms, the Big Room and the playing fields, tie askew, coattails flapping, as tangible and real as if he were alive.

Already, in 1929, there were many who said Old Sawney's school was an anachronism. It still required a boy to study four years of Latin and two of Greek before Son Will, chipped from the same block, would say you were ready for college. For the rest, you studied only history, English literature and composition, mathematics and, if you insisted, physics. No modern languages, no social studies, no current events, and of course no "practical" courses in bookkeeping, business or carpentry.

The methodology was as quaint as the curriculum. Whatever you studied, you took it straight. Caesar was as Caesar wrote with no simplification of vocabulary or subjunctives; so with your Shakespeare, Dickens or Emerson. You studied Homer as both Greek and poetry; there are Old Boys today who, with a drink under their belt, can rattle off the first thirty or forty lines of the *Iliad* with hardly a stumble. Mathematics meant not just simple algebra but trigonometry and the calculus, and this years before "advanced placement" studies in high school were ever thought of. The physics course would make an educator's hair curl. Nobody took time heating up rods to measure the coefficient of expansion; you could look that up in a book, which was what books were for. But you had the principles of physics drummed into your head, and before you were through Galileo and Newton were old friends.

Furthermore, you were expected to know and not almost know. The slow learner was met with much patience, the bright boy who was lazy or sloppy with none at all. If you got an "A" you knew you deserved it; the grading system wasn't "relative." Sometimes in some classes there would be no "A's" at all; I remember at least one trigonometry class in which everybody got an "A," because I made it and was still at the foot of the class.

If bad work was penalized, good work was rewarded and the top students—not the athletes—were the privileged in this quaint and closed society. Old Sawney had accumulated an enormous number of seemingly silly rules for the boys. For example, a junior wasn't allowed to set foot on the grounds around the senior classroom and vice-versa; you weren't allowed to stop on the path in moving from one class to another; and so on. But a boy who made all "A's" was exempt from all these rules, he could (and did) lord it over his fellows. This was one of the ways Sawney devised to put a premium upon excellence.

But, in the heritage from Old Sawney, excellence was a thing not limited to classroom studies. He knew that not every boy was equal in intelligence and therefore not every boy could achieve classroom excellence. So long after he was gone the school still considered its first task the building of character; the will to do the best one could, the courage to be honest not only with one's fellows but with one-self. And this meant discipline, imposed at first from the outside until in time it could be imposed from within.

Discipline, nowadays, has become a dirty word. To most people it implies, almost exclusively, corporal punishment for misbehavior. It meant that to Old Sawney, too, and many an old Webb boy can remember having his palm whacked for his misdeeds. But it also meant a great deal more. It meant, when you are studying Greek, getting the diacritical marks correct. It meant, when asked to do an English composition of 368 words, writing precisely 368 words, neither one more nor one less. It meant disciplining your-self to do the day's assignment on your own time at your own pace. It also meant disciplining yourself not to cheat when the temptation was there, partly because it was unfair to the other boys competing with you but mostly because it was unfair to yourself.

Thus there was a curious paradox about the discipline for which Old Sawney's school became famous—and, to some, infamous. There was the corporal punishment. There was the short-shrift for those who misbehaved. There was the intolerance of sloppy work. But there was also an intoxicating freedom within the disciplined framework.

On a nice day the boys could choose to have their classes out of doors, reading Cicero under a tree. Class over in the afternoon, they were free to do as they would, study if they felt like it, play football if they wished, roam the countryside at their pleasure. At night only the most laggard scholars had formal study hall. The others could loaf the night away or burn the midnight oil as the spirit moved them. You were expected to be prepared, but how and when you prepared was your own decision. At exam time the teacher put the questions on the blackboard and departed; the penalty for cheating was draconian, the responsibility entirely your own.

If such a school at such a time seemed to many already out of date in 1929, it was in its beginnings both radical and experimental. Not so much in its curriculum, for ever since the earliest American "prep" schools—Andover in 1778 and Exeter in 1781—the study programs had leaned heavily on the classical languages, borrowing their basic curriculum from the English "public" schools. What made Old Sawney an educational radical was his attitude toward his school and the boys who came there.

The post–Civil War period was the flourishing time for prep schools; in the East they sprang up everywhere. St. Marks was founded in 1865, Groton in 1884, Taft in 1890, and Choate in 1896. But they were seeded in a time and place of prosperity and on the eve of a still more booming era in New England. There the new mercantile and banking classes were being born, and as families grew prosperous—especially those of English descent—they looked to the home country for models of the schools to send their sons. They were good models and they resulted in exceedingly good schools. But the very prosperity which made them blossom also gave them a very special character; they tended, as the years passed, to become schools for the sons of the rich and the well-born. Endicott Peabody of Groton, the archtypical headmaster of the New England prep schools, was family-connected with J. P. Morgan and a graduate himself of an English public school, and he put that stamp on his school and those like it.

The post–Civil War South was something else again, and so was young Sawney Webb. Being a conquered land it was an impoverished area. Sawney's own education had come in fits and starts, twice interrupted by service in the Confederate army. When the Reconstruction period came, he was without fortune or, seemingly, without future.

How this remarkable man came to Bell Buckle and wrought what he wrought there is the story of this book. What is worth noting here is how the time and circumstances put a different cast upon Webb School, for all its similarities with the eastern prep schools.

Like the eastern schools it was, of course, elitist in outlook because Sawney intended it to be a place for educating those who would go on to college and become the leaders of the South. But circumstances barred it from being a school for the rich; in the South of 1886 there were few such. So of necessity the school became much more democratic in its admissions policies. Sawney was more interested in the boys themselves, in their own capabilities, than in their family backgrounds or the material wealth of their families. To a shy new boy embarrassed by his family's poverty and lack of education, Sawney remarked, "I want you to go into the world and pedigree your ancestors."

This difference in circumstance was reflected in a number of ways. For one, Webb School never went in for uniforms or even for expecting the boys to be "dressed up." If a youngster had a suit for Sunday, that was all the formal clothes he needed. Even in my own time, when prosperity had come to the school and most of the student body came from well-to-do families, the usual dress was corduroy trousers, shirts, and sweaters.

It also affected the way Sawney spent the school's money. When he raised $12,000 to start the school (a considerable sum for those times), he spent little of his initial capital on buildings but $8,000 on books. Years later it took all the persuasion of Son Will, who followed his father as headmaster, and of the board of trustees to persuade the old man to spend money on such extravagances as dormitories. He would have much preferred to have enlarged the library.

The fact that Sawney himself had an interrupted education, marked by some very bad schools and some inspirational teachers, had its effect too. It made him put a high value on education itself, and gave him a contempt for anything shoddy about the process, whether on the part of the teacher or the pupil. He knew how hard a good education was to come by and what a difference it could make in a man's life; he meant the boys to earn it and value it.

So another paradox. If to some Old Sawney's school seemed, already in 1929, out of date, some of it also seems quite advanced even at this date. "Learn one thing at a time," he said, "that's all Solomon could do," which is not a bad description of programmed learning, to use the modern phrase. "Great masses of students," he said another time, "tend to become a machine with lesson hearers and no teachers"—a remark that ought to be appreciated by those students today complaining about the vast, impersonal nature of our modern educational system.

And what of this? "Before I imprison innocent children," he once said, "I would quit the profession of teaching. . . . A child ought to love to go to school."

Not all of them loved it at Sawney's school. Many of them were sent home because they couldn't make it, some fled because they couldn't take it. I myself hated it at first; I had, at 15, already graduated from a public high school where almost right was good enough, and by that Christmas, 1929, I was ready to go home and stay. What difference did it make if I confused an ablative with an accusative after a Latin preposition, or if I wanted to use three more words to say what I wanted to say in an English composition? Not all the boys who knew him, so I gather, loved Old Sawney himself; he could be mean, cantankerous, and a petty tyrant.

But what is the measure of a schoolmaster? One, surely, is what his boys do thereafter. The list of Sawney's Old Boys who went on to be senators, governors, leaders in this industry or that, lawyers, doctors, teachers, or even editors, is long enough to grow tiresome. In its first fifty years, for whatever this may say of the teaching there, Sawney's school provided more Rhodes scholars than any other American secondary school.

Yet this is not the only, or maybe even the best, measure of a schoolmaster; every school has its distinguished alumni and it is not easy to be sure whether the school distinguished them or they the school. Henry Adams thought that a good teacher affected eternity because one can never tell where his influence stops. If eternity is hardly measurable, still it is worth noting that Sawney Webb has been dead over fifty years and yet his ghost still walks. At last count, there are at least five schools all over the country, headed by his descendants or his apostles, in which the Sawney tradition lives on.

There are, of course, those who say that tradition itself is an anachronism. The small private school is under attack, the cult of excellence is criticized in the name of democracy, the inculcation of character and will, or the desire to learn merely for learning's sake, is not supposed to be the teacher's task. The cry in many quarters is for education to be egalitarian—that is, the same for everybody—and above all to be "relevant." Nothing is deader in pedagogy than dead languages.

It is true that even in Bell Buckle things are not as they used to be. The Big Room has yielded to the modern auditorium and the attractive campus is dotted with brick and mortar. Most of Sawney's "silly" rules are gone. So too is the Greek, and even Latin, as befits the new day, is optional. As one who had his share of both languages, I will not weep for that; anyway I have forgotten most of each. But to think these changes outmode Sawney Webb mistakes the mannerisms for the manner.

In that Bell Buckle of long ago, Latin and Greek were not taught as ends in themselves; no one pretended that an ability to read the *Iliad* was going to be useful in the practical world, although an acquaintance with it is not without its value. Latin and Greek were tools to toughen young minds; cleverness and a gift of gab will not get you through Ciceronian syntax. Sawney used them because they were the tools of his time, but it was the training of minds that interested him, not what was stuffed into them.

Thomas Huxley once wrote that the most valuable result of all education is the ability to make yourself do what you have to do, when it ought to be done, whether you like it or not. Sawney would have agreed, but with the proviso that you not only do it but do it to the best of your ability; half best would not do. His aim, he once said, was "to develop those powers of the mind which tend to distinguish rather than reduce to a 'contemptible dead level.' "

How well he succeeded with those who came under his sway can only be answered personally, each man for himself. I confess that with myself his reach exceeded a boy's grasp, but—and I am not alone—I came to love Sawney's school because I found there teachers who wanted to give me a love of learning, a pride in doing. That, surely, is a schoolmaster's tradition not without relevance now to our troubled times.

VERMONT ROYSTER

Acknowledgments

A book is far more than the labor of one human being. Footnotes are the formal expression of scholarly indebtedness. These acknowledgments are my less formal way of giving thanks.

The following institutions contributed their scholarship and time to my twenty-year effort to document this biography: the Southern Historical Collection of the University of North Carolina Library at Chapel Hill, whose Webb family letters and documents alone contain a regional saga of intense human interest; the Webb School in the historic village of Bell Buckle, whose personnel unearthed significant photographs and memorabilia; the Tennessee State Archives at Nashville, from which I was able to gather obscure details about Webb's early Culleoka days, and where Colonel Campbell Brown, historical consultant, gave me help; the Tennessee Historical Society; the library of the Methodist Publishing House, Nashville, which furnished records of Sawney Webb's leadership in church affairs; Princeton University, where archives and alumni files substantiate the tradition that Webb-Bell Buckle alumni were instrumental in establishing Princeton's Honor System; the Manuscript Collection of the Vanderbilt University Library, where I read John Maurice Webb's letters to Edwin Mims; the New York Public Library, the New-York Historical Society Library, and a New York City Department of Corrections tour of Hart's Island, sources of data that corroborate Sawney Webb's account of his Civil War capture and imprisonment; the Hall of Fame of the Trotter (and pacer) in Goshen, New York, where I researched the harness-racing history behind the fable of the Little Brown Jug; the Library of Congress, where I gathered information about Sawney Webb's days in the United States Senate; the North Carolina State Archives, which have preserved additional Webb family letters; the Nashville Public Library, where I consulted old *American, Banner,* and *Tennessean* files; the Goodwyn Institute and Cossitt Libraries at Memphis, where the research began, and Honnold Library of the Claremont (California) University Center, where research first took a coherent shape.

Among the published books I found particularly helpful are Donald Davidson's *The Tennessee: The New River, Civil War to TVA* (New York, 1948), which introduced me to Sawney Webb; the biographical essay on Old Sawney in Edd Winfield Parks's *Segments of Southern Thought* (Athens, Ga., 1938), which in a footnote emphasized the need for a biography, and which appeared in its original form as "Sawney Webb: Tennessee's Schoolmaster" in Volume XII, Number 3, of the *North Carolina Historical Review* (July, 1935); John Andrew Rice's *I Came Out of the Eighteenth Century* (New York, 1942) for its sensitive tribute to John Webb and to the school Old Sawney founded and governed; Edwin Mims's "John Maurice Webb (1847–1916)," published in *Webb School in Celebration of its 75th Anniversary* (Bell Buckle, 1945); Paul Barringer's *The Natural Bent* (Chapel Hill, N.C., 1949), for an impression of the old Bingham School and of William Bingham in particular, and for its account of the experiences of Dr. Barringer's father, General Rufus Barringer, and of Sawney Webb when they were prisoners of war together; W. J. Webb's *Our Webb Kin of Dixie* (privately published in Oxford, N.C., 1940), for its remarkably accurate and thorough information; W. O. Batts's *Private Preparatory Schools for Boys in Tennessee* (privately published in Columbia, Tennessee [?], 1957); and Robert Hiram White's *Development of the Tennessee State Educational Organization, 1796–1929* (Nashville, 1929), which graphically describes the deplorable educational conditions following the Civil War.

Among a number of significant newspaper stories, two need special acknowledgment: the remarkable history of the Webb Tower, in the January 2, 1927, edition of the *Asheville Citizen*, and " 'Sawney' Webb and the 'Only Don't in his Gospel of Do' " in the January 13, 1912, edition of the *Nashville Banner*, whose present publisher James G. Stahlman has done much to foster the traditions of his old teacher.

I am especially grateful to the surviving children of Sawney Webb: Dr. Thompson Webb, Mrs. Susan Webb Price, and Mrs. Emma Webb McLean of Claremont, California, for allowing me access to their collections, and for their interviews; to Mrs. Emma Webb Steed of Los Angeles, a granddaughter, for her bright and vivid memories; and to their kinsman, the late Bruce Webb of Asheville, North Carolina, for his help and perceptive interest in my project. I am indebted to Edward T. Price, a son-in-law, and a onetime teacher at Bell Buckle and founder of the old Price-Webb school at Lewisburg, Tennessee; to Vivian Howell Webb of Claremont, helpmate of the founder of the second Webb School; to the late Adeline Webb Sibley of Vista, California; and to the late W. R. Webb, Jr., Old Sawney's eldest son and successor at Bell Buckle, for hours of interviews and recollections.

I am likewise grateful to the surviving daughter of John M. Webb, Miss Cornelia Webb of Lynchburg, Virginia; to Dr. John M. Webb II, grandson, and dean of men at the University of the South, Sewanee; to the late Dr. Albert Webb of Durham, North Carolina, John Webb's son; and to Dr. Albert G. Sanders of Jackson, Mississippi, for helpful cooperation in supplying both insight and information about the scholar-principal of Bell Buckle.

I also recall with the deepest pleasure interviews with scores of onetime student "sons and daughters": two Culleoka alumni, the late T. Leigh Thompson of Lewisburg, and the late Augustus Henry Hatcher, of Fayetteville, Tennessee, both of whom I visited in 1952 when the former was 97 and the latter 103; a Culleoka alumna, the late Mrs. Clabie Taylor Graham, daughter of Sawney Webb's lifetime best friends; Bell Buckle alumni, including the late Webb Follin, one of Old Sawney's successors as principal; the late former Governor Prentice Cooper of Shelbyville, Tennessee; the late Marshall McDonald of Macon, Mississippi; and John T. Clary of Huntsville, Alabama, Webb kinsman, and onetime student and teacher.

My interview with the late John Willis Hays of Oxford, North Carolina, belongs in a special category for its details of Oxford's Horner School days, which might otherwise have been lost or mislaid.

A number of unpublished manuscripts have contributed to this volume. Most important among them are the lengthy biographical tribute by the Reverend Josiah Sibley, Old Sawney's late son-in-law, which I mined heavily; the notebook of sketches about Sawney Webb's childhood and a monograph on the man's influence by his eldest daughter and sometime secretary, the late Alla Webb; also, the schoolboy notes of Old Sawney's Big Room lectures by the late Reverend Raymond Browning, and the late General T. A. Frazier of Chattanooga; accounts of Culleoka by Elliston Farrell and W. H. Witt; an "unforgettable character" sketch by Edwin T. Vaughn, and other Bell Buckle sketches in the memoirs of the late

Reverend C. A. Waterfield of Nashville, and Phillips Andover's late master of the classics, Horace Poynter.

This book has a host of friends, individuals whose professional judgments reinforced my will: Dr. Emory Stevens Bucke of Nashville; Dr. Herbert W. Schneider and Dr. Richard Armour of Claremont; the late Dr. Douglass Adair, head of the history department of the Claremont Graduate School and University Center, whose patient guidance on my master's thesis, *Sawney Webb: Southern Schoolmaster, A Case History of Individualism in American Education*, laid scholarly foundations for this volume; and Dr. James Welch Patton of Chapel Hill, who brought his encyclopedic knowledge of southern history to bear on my scholarship by thoughtfully reading both my thesis and my manuscript for judgment and accuracy.

My deepest gratitude also goes to Bell Buckle alumni Walter Stokes, Jr., of Nashville, indispensable friend of the book and discriminating admirer of its subject; Dr. William Y. Elliott of Washington, D.C., for contributions of ideas as well as personal memories; and onetime trustee and former principal at Bell Buckle, Henry O. Whiteside, and his wife Emma, for their help and kindness.

I am indebted to John M. Allen, senior staff editor of *Reader's Digest*, for timely encouragement and guidance in my writing of the first chapter; friend, colleague, and bookman Gerald Johnson of the Webb School of California, Claremont, for his critical and perceptive reading of the manuscript; novelist Charlotte Edwards of Oxford, Maryland, for contagious enthusiasm and timely tips; novelist Robert Richards of Memphis for early belief; artist and cartoonist Frank Adams of Skyforest, California, for his encouraging advice on the manuscript in progress; Thurston and Janet Jordan for their confidence throughout the writing year of 1968–1969, during those months that the California mountains were supposed to collapse into the Pacific Ocean; the late Mrs. Louise Kelly of Skyforest; helpful librarians at the Lake Arrowhead Branch of the San Bernardino County Public Library; and Headmaster Frederick R. Hooper, Master Teacher Raymond M. Alf, both of Claremont, and the late Dean John R. C. Sumner, benefactors, beneficiaries, and exemplars of the best in the Webb tradition.

I must acknowledge intellectual and aesthetic debts to Robert Henri, American artist and teacher, for his inspirational advice in

The Art Spirit (New York, 1960), summed up in the sentence, "Motive demands specific technique," which helped me reduce a book moving toward fifteen hundred pages to one of fewer than two hundred; to William Faulkner for vital words about mankind from his Nobel Prize acceptance speech, which I found essential to the expression of my theme; to Dylan Thomas for a phrase from "Do Not Go Gentle Into That Good Night," which I used to open the concluding chapter; and to Catherine Drinker Bowen, whose *Biography: The Craft and the Calling* (Boston, 1969) I tried to live by and follow in my writing.

The Webb–Bell Buckle Board of Trustees, with the cooperation of the Webb of California Board, made it possible for me to complete research and write this book. My students for fifteen academic years have been resource persons from whom I feel I have learned more than I could have taught them.

My wife has been my partner and companion in all the work of this book except the writing, and in that she has been a most helpful critic.

Last of all, I should like to express my appreciation to the staff of The University of North Carolina Press for the considerate care and attention they have given to transforming my manuscript into a published book.

None of the men and women mentioned above is to blame for what follows, but if there is any merit in it, they gave the author essential help.

One word of explanation about dialogue and direct quotations: none of them is my invention, although some of them are recollections of alumni, Sawney Webb himself, and other memoir-makers. In the few places where I have pieced together bits of memory in the oral tradition so as to suggest a plausible restoration, the text clearly indicates their approximate character.

—LAURENCE McMILLIN

The Schoolmaker

*The upbringing of the human being
must lead both intelligence and will
toward achievement, and the shaping of
the intellect. Yet, whereas the educational system of schools and colleges
succeeds as a rule in equipping men's
intellect for knowledge, it seems to be
missing its main achievement, the equipping of man's will. What an infelicity!*

—JACQUES MARITAIN
Education at the Crossroads, 1943

*There used to be problems of courage,
honor, chastity, virtue . . . they don't exist any more. There are only 'angles.' . . .
Some day we'll run out of angles and have
to get back to virtues.*

—WILLIAM FAULKNER
Associated Press Interview, 1950

*Modern man is not as virile as he
used to be. Instead of making things happen, he waits for things to happen to him.
He goes with the current. Something in our
society has led him to stop fighting, to
cease swimming upstream. . . .
I remember my grandfather. He lived to
be 90. I used to watch him and admire his
authority. Where has all that gone? What's
happened to that kind of man?*

—MARCELLO MASTROIANNI
Interview in *Playboy,* 1965

I. Foreglimpses

If I pick up a book
about a man's life
and it tells me nothing
about his boyhood,
I lay it aside.
—SAWNEY WEBB

No road led to High Windy. No horse and wagon, even, had struggled within miles of the place. In 1916 students erected a lookout tower there. They carried steel bars and cement by mulepack and by sledge. They applied climb, sweat, spring water, and devotion. Then they named their finished work for a living man who had made a fifty-year career of fatherhood.

Thousands of young people for ten summers thereafter followed the steep trail, to watch in silence from the tower as the peaks of the North Carolina Blue Ridge emerged from the mystic night, and to sing hymns of praise upon the tower as the youthful sun sprang up. They stumbled over roots and stones and fallen trees. They rested their feet on banks of green galax leaves and fern. They kept moving upward, sometimes on hands and knees. There was no easy way.

On the bleak Sunday of December 26, 1926, a hiking party from the lodge at Blue Ridge community found a good reason to climb on up to High Windy summit after tracing a little mountain stream to its source. Now they were scrambling over frozen ground, through naked briars and across icy torrents, slipping on the stones, grasping roots and branches. They expected no view from the tower on this lowering winter's day. But some of them had heavy hearts and a sad purpose because the old man for whom the tower had been named was dead.

At last the tower came into view. A weird silhouette was stooping against the cold gray sky. The platform atop the 30-foot skeleton of steel was wrenched from its place, hanging to one side in mid-air. To the awe-struck witnesses, Webb Tower was bowing its head in grief. A hunter, they learned, had seen the tower intact the day before Old Sawney Webb passed away.

The end of his 84-year adventure made news across the continent, evoked long obituaries of praise as far away as St. Louis, put eight-column headlines on the front pages of Tennessee dailies, and brought a fast train to a special stop at his tiny home village of Bell Buckle the rainy day of his funeral.

He was the child of a doomed society. In his youth he watched the American government failing. He lived out his young manhood with violence, and felt his world, like his cavalry horse, shot out from under him.

Then he became a teacher where good schools were virtually non-existent. From fragments of his half-wrecked heritage, he improvised a portable society from the most unpromising beginnings in the moldy basement of a church. This educational society—this unique school community—endured and prevailed over the chaotic change and stagnation that might have destroyed it, even as he survived, and endured, and prevailed.

A hundred years ago, his private institution was open to young people of all creeds, and of all races, with the tragic exception of one. In spite of the specific racism that the outrage of prolonged revolutionary violence had imposed on him, he believed in a family of man—and practiced his belief within the limits that the patched but unhealed southern society tolerated.

Here was an education according to nature, and a respect for the human species as the purposeful creature of earth. Two years before a youth named John Dewey received his bachelor's degree, Sawney Webb was warning the National Education Association in a speech: "To crowd great multitudes of children together and to require of them that perfect order which is described by its advocates by the term clockwork, and to require of them to sit at their desks when they can do better work under a tree, to exact of everyone at the same time the same motions is not like a family, nor is it natural, nor does it tend to develop those powers of the mind which distinguish rather than reduce to a 'contemptible dead level.' " To his sorrow, he occasionally saw "mechanical" teaching in some of the best-known schools of New York and Boston, and watched as the unhappy children went through their lessons "with a sigh."

In full life he came striding out of the nineteenth century, coat-tails flying so that boys said you could play marbles on them—bearing a more striking resemblance each year to his idol, Robert E. Lee. His wide eyes of crockery blue leaped about restlessly as if ready to thrust loose from their sockets. He made his presence felt in the Big Room, along the gravel path, in his campus "office" out under beech branches—and even in the United States Senate. "The scholar is not the mechanically taught but the personally inspired. . . . Great masses of students tend to become a machine with lesson hearers and no teachers," he warned his fellow senators in early 1913.

As long as he lived, his independent school withstood the impersonal tyranny of Big Education's inflexible standards. He deplored the trend, old even in his own day, to build a pedagogical practice on industrial metaphors.

A longtime U.S. commissioner of education, college president, and academic leader, John Tigert, who had gone to school to him, said near the end of his life about the old teacher, "I would venture to assert that he had a finer perception of boys and their nature than anyone else I have ever known, with a possible exception of Mark Twain."

The schoolmaster was unorthodox and controversial. He talked, inspired, joked, encouraged, fought, praised, denounced, excited, scorned, challenged, wrestled, heckled, scared, whipped (on the hand), laughed, nudged, teased, shamed, surprised, pushed, begged, and even bored boys into forsaking ignorance—into learning and wanting to learn. He insisted he ran the school on wit and wisdom.

He dealt with different boys in differing ways. He practiced an education of daily confrontations. He required thorough, rigorous intellectual work. He also brought spontaneity to the school experience. He was a master of homegrown Zen insights. He turned the generation gap of his own times into a game. He knew how to make people laugh.

He adhered to an almost forgotten notion, taught by a number of history's wisest men, that self-enslavement is freedom's greatest enemy. He did not regard scholarship as tantamount to the human virtues—which he called "character." He passionately believed that the schooling of men, even if it risked being overdone, was crucial to human progress and survival. He knew "his boys" too well to equate their juvenile honesty with wisdom. He loved them too well to make a cowardly surrender to their wills. He ascribed to them as individuals the highest value on the earth. "My son," he would say to one boy or to an audience of hundreds, *"Don't do things on the sly!"*

The schoolmaker prevailed over war, famine, physical disability, social chaos, political disorder, and a variety of plagues. As a 130-pound war veteran with a lame right arm, he began running into opposition that eventually broke out into violence. He "accomplished amazing results with such little equipment that he shames the rest of us," wrote Horace Taft, founder of the Taft School in Connecticut, about Old Sawney. Yet he had never wanted a career in the school room at all.

The natural-born teacher was his brilliant younger brother. Quiet Old Jack Webb with the wisdom bump on his high forehead was a gentle omnivore of books who mumbled in several languages as, head down, he walked Bell Buckle's streets. Students loved him for his lifetime friendship and inspiration, and university professors deferred to him for his comprehensive learning. The older brother knew the school's academic distinction owed most to Old Jack's work.

The bearded brothers Webb, who looked physically much alike, were a unique team of opposites. Their school enjoyed, and suffered, a variety of paradoxical reputations. Some heard it was a school of last resort for delinquents in their teens, the last private hope for the parents of young incorrigibles.

Enemies described the school as a nightmare-come-true out of the troubled childhood memories of highly imaginative novelists, in which a bearded ogre flogged and thrashed his tender young victim into submission. Parents, in fact, were known to use Old Sawney's name as a threat to their disobedient little boys. Some people to this day mistakenly think of Webb School as a boys' reformatory. Others knew from experience that it was different. It graduated young men trusted throughout the academic world for never lying or cheating. It was the home of an uncompromising code of honor, where students themselves asked young violators to leave.

Boys ran their own study halls and learned together noisily outdoors. Seventy-five years before advanced placement they were encouraged, not pressured, to move on to college as fast as their willing ability could carry them. They won surprise holidays to roam the countryside, or to ice skate with girl students of the village. Webb was a learning community of non-violent ideals. A respect for all living things was both a rule and a custom. This school put human development ahead of scholarship.

Yet Woodrow Wilson heard from his university faculty that some of Princeton's best-prepared students came from this quaint educational enterprise with the practice of ignoring the changing fads of pedagogy. Later, several Webb alumni were playing key roles in President Wilson's national administration. During a surprise conversation he told one of them he considered Webb about the best preparatory school in the nation. Webb graduates had been chiefly responsible for Princeton's honor code, which became known as the Princeton System.

Before its fiftieth birthday, Webb–Bell Buckle counted more Rhodes scholars among its graduates than any other secondary school. Harvard, as well as Oxford in England, recognized the superiority of this boarding school without dormitories in a village that had grown up as a shipping point for livestock on the Nashville & Chattanooga Railroad. Bell Buckle was a cattle town with intellectual sophistication. Here a parrot recited Greek and a cow caught mistakes in Latin.

The school inspired and generated many others, one as far away as California, and peopled with faculties the lagging public school movement of the South. Yet its graduating classes seldom reached thirty in number, and frequently amounted to fewer than ten. Old Sawney himself took the stump for all schools, public as well as private, for any schools but shams. He carried on a personal antipoverty program for rural youth, fired their aspiration, and kept it burning.

The Webb–Bell Buckle story actually begins in the red hills of upper North Carolina two decades before the Civil War. The flexible traditions of educational independence out of which it grew are as old as 1793, yet remain alive to change in the 1970s. It is the story of a remarkable schoolmaking family and a remarkable family-type school—two human institutions that have generally lost the most ground under the social pressures of the past century. It is the spiritual account of an undaunted father figure who paid the price of loneliness, misunderstanding, and disbelief for his efforts to equip "his boys" to endure and master change. His vigorous contempt for adults who abandoned children to their untrained impulses did not endear him even in his old age to a generation thoughtlessly committed to instant pleasure and quick riches.

The plot itself is too improbable to have become the basis of a novel. As always, the plot belongs to the man of action. A story of danger and courage, it is touched with tragedy and hope. It persists as a memory, and it illustrates the promise that mankind can survive and prevail.

II. I'm from God's Great Kindergarten

Sometimes I go
to some of those schools in the city
and the teacher shows me a little glass bowl
with some stalks of wheat growing in it
and maybe another bowl
with some tadpoles
and some pictures on the wall
and they call that kindergarten.
  I'm from the country,
God's great kindergarten,
where a boy can walk
through fields of waving grain
and wade knee deep in tadpoles.
—SAWNEY WEBB

He was born in a New World farmhouse on November 11, 1842, only a few months after the most famous English-speaking schoolmaster, Thomas Arnold of Rugby, had died in Old World Oxford. He grew up to be praised as the Arnold of America.

A more picturesque identity settled on him before he was christened. Alexander Smith Webb and Cornelia Adeline Stanford Webb found it hard to name their fifth son. The next youngest son lisped the suggestion "Tawney" and the family changed it to

"Sawney." That was Sister Susan's recollection, and she helped to raise the little boy.

The fifth son himself chose to remember it differently. "My father called me 'Sawney.' Sawney is a term of endearment in Scotland for the name Alexander, and my brother just older than I being called Alexander, I suppose when I came he wanted another namesake."

It strengthens a son to believe he was special to his father, especially to a father he scarcely knew. Yet his nickname made him uncomfortable for three decades. He tried to move away from "Sawney" three times, and three times "Sawney" came traveling after him. Only after the lessons of brutal years did he learn to make the most and best of it. His Christian name was recorded in the big Bible as William Robert. Very early he began to insist that his real name was William.

Alexander and Adeline Webb named his first home Harmony Hill. Immediately to their east rose a high hill known as Mount Tirzah, which took its name from an Indian word for beautiful. Their fifth son began his life in Person County, not far from the southern border of Old Virginia.

Sawney's father was as anxious as his times. His gentle wideset eyes had the gaze of a man who saw he had too much to do at once. His jaw was strong, but the corners of his mouth were drawn. Alexander's thin body was wearing out fast. Younger brothers tempted him with tall accounts of the fat new lands of the Western country. They briskly invited him to cross the Alleghenies. "If your wife will not agree to come, you must pack up everything and start, leaving a horse hitched at the rack with a saddle on it, and she will be sure to follow."

In 1845, Alexander Webb did pack up everything, but he moved fewer than fifty miles—south by west. Sawney was too young to remember living at his birthplace, or leaving it behind. Yet the move affected his future as no other event in his infancy or childhood. It also settled the future of his unborn brother John. The large family and their "servants" bounced and jostled over deep-rutted red dirt roads through the Carolina hills. They took horse and carriage, oxen and wagon, the paraphernalia of a domestic enterprise that must do virtually everything for themselves. (The family never called their human property "slaves.")

They reached the small cluster of frame buildings at the Oaks community, passed the Binghams' newly acquired farm and academy buildings on the left, crossed the road that led to the university at Chapel Hill—woods again—then Bethlehem Church in a clearing on the right with the rock-laden yard around it and a small cemetery. A quarter of a mile farther south, they turned into a drive before a two-story frame house at the bottom of a "mountain field." A great cluster of oaks shaded the front yard. Gray granite littered the dell. This was Stony Point.

Sawney's infant memory began to take hold here. Yet his father was never more for him than a shadowy figure. He did know that his father took him once to an election. "I was a little one and I remember very well his holding me up in his arms among the men, patting me on the head, and saying, 'Here is a Henry Clay Whig.' " Sawney also remembered standing by his father in the orchard and watching him plant an apple tree. He never forgot the earnestness in Alexander's words, "My son, I don't expect to live long enough to eat fruit from this tree, but fix it in your mind and heart that you must do something that will be an aid to those that follow after us, and that are here after we are gone."

One day, the frail little man-child tried his own experiment in moral earnestness. He charged like a giant-killer out of the Webb yard at Stony Point, and attacked a country acquaintance with a stick. The man disarmed his puny adversary and hung him, kicking and squalling furiously, by the scruff of his little homespun shirt on a fence paling. Older Webbs answered the boy's shrill cries. But why had he been so wicked as to act so violently?

Sawney explained that the man was wicked. He had heard his mother and father describe him so. Mother tried to teach her little son to make his attacks on evil more civilized. She said about anyone of whom she disapproved, "Poor fellow, he does not know any better." Father also knew the hazards of ignorance, but his health was now declining rapidly. "My daughter, teach my children," he said, almost in desperation, to Susan, his second eldest girl.

His belief that the future belonged to education was the principle of his practical design. He pieced together 460 acres around Stony Point, placed his growing family in an inadequate house, started raising log outbuildings as fast as he could—including a two-story dormitory and a kitchen—brought two young boarders into the crowded frame house within months after the move, and put his three eldest daughters through boarding school in Hillsboro. Harmony Hill with its hundreds of acres remained unsold. For a man with a reputation for good business sense, Father Webb seemed guilty of the greatest economic foolishness. He refused, however, to give his highest priority to the American dollar.

Schools of quality were non-existent around Harmony Hill, but less than a mile from Stony Point there now stood one of the South's finest academies. Parents sent their sons hundreds of miles to study with W. J. Bingham. This "Napoleon of Schoolmasters" had decided in 1844 to move to Oaks, "with special reference to the education of his own sons in the country."

Here as Webb sons reached their teens, they could attend the celebrated school as day students. James, the eldest, enrolled immediately. The family also accommodated Schoolmaster Bingham by taking in students as boarders. Bingham needed families of character to play host to student "sons," and be jointly responsible for their behavior out of school. Sawney began his conscious life as a member of a large school family in a boarding school community as did his future partner, Brother John.

Time for their frail father at last ran out. In 1848 he made his will, a year later he named James executor, and on June 30, 1849, he was dead at forty-seven. Sawney was just old enough to remember what his boyhood had lost. He felt and absorbed his mother's grief. It was three days before Adeline Webb's thirty-eighth birthday. She was carrying her twelfth child. Of the ten other surviving children, James was not quite twenty-one, but his formal education had to end. John Maurice Webb, born November 29, 1847, was barely nineteen months old. Sawney himself was only six-and-a-half.

It was strange to lose a loved one in June, usually the warm emblem of happy days, and the promise of increasing life. With her husband buried in nearby Bethlehem churchyard, the Widow Webb could take no time for further mourning. Only throbbing migraine headaches made her rest. She faced a man's job of running the entire establishment—hundreds of acres—much of it fifty horse-and-buggy miles away. She was responsible for the feeding and clothing of forty human beings of two races as well as feeding and housing six to eight boarders forty weeks a year. Most of the food and much of the clothing had to come from her land and animals. It was an all-around farm. Her children as well as the servants supplied the labor.

The widow gave birth to Sam in late October. Adeline was not robust, but she was strong. Her firm lips drew deepening creases, matching the lines that gathered in her forehead. She parted her chestnut hair, and brushed it straight. She wore a copious scarf on her head, and tied it under her determined chin. "I shall never forget the brightness of her face and the warm grasp of my hand with both of hers and her moist eyes as she said, 'Oh, I am so glad to see you,' " a frequent visitor said, and she had many. Adeline's widowed mother lived with her. Both drew comfort from their faith, which promised reunions beyond the grave. Servants Doc or Stephen, wearing brass button livery, drove them to church in a carriage, or as the simpler neighbors called it, the "Sunday wagon."

Sawney would learn to read to his own student "sons" from the life of his early boyhood. "My mother used to say to me with so much emphasis, 'My son, if you are polite to the Queen and rude to the servant that blacks your boots, you are not a gentleman. You are a fraud and a sham.' . . . I was tied to my mother's apron strings. I hope to be tied to her apron strings throughout eternity."

In his home Sawney found another "big personality," a girl still in her teens, the greatest teacher he said he ever knew. Susan, or "Suny," knew more than anyone else. Sawney watched her on Saturday at the dining room fireplace, baking perfect bread in "oven" pots on short legs in hot coals. Depressed lids held glowing ashes on top for even heat. Cakes, biscuits, and roast ducks emerged from similar pots, while other meats turned on spits over the glowing wood fire. Suny and Black Nancy even made waffles in molds with tong-like handles, the batter ends thrust deep in ashes. Stony Point was often a place of fragrant smells.

Suny never did wrong. She always placed her knife and fork neatly on her plate, and folded her napkin while she was still a bit hungry. She never allowed her back to touch her chair. She very much resembled a good straight pen. Suny wrote hundreds and thousands of letters. She became the corresponding secretary of the family. She loved putting English words together. She dressed to suit herself—no trails, no silly outsized bustles for her. She remained too busy at the vocation her father had left her to give her full heart to courting though admirers called on her from a distance. Suny never married.

My daughter, teach my children. She did teach them, and some of their children, and neighbors' children, for forty years. She began teaching Sawney no later than the summer of 1848, and formally opened her school four months before her father died. She charged a nickel a day, a quarter a week, per child.

The log building daubed with mud that became "Almeda School-house" sat on the partially wooded slopes of the mountain field. The day began with a Bible passage, which her students read along with her as best they could. After a prayer, she taught.

"All day long in the little log cabin I sat by my little chum in a seat when our feet did not touch the floor," Sawney remembered. Even fifteen minutes was uncomfortable on backless puncheon benches, logs split or sawed in half, with the flat end to sit on. "We could not move our feet, and we were not allowed to speak a word." Her discipline was rigid. Yet she knew that a child has limits. "When she saw that her pupils were tired she would tell a story or read a beautiful poem. I never saw a little boy leave her school that did not have a love of poetry and good English." Sawney learned about Br'er Rabbit and the Tar Baby, although the rich folklore of the blacks had not yet made a white journalist famous. Long division was the biggest puzzle of his life.

Little girls swept the rough floor, and little boys fetched drinking water from the spring. It was a downhill run northwest toward the house, and a climbing return with heavy oaken buckets. Sawney enjoyed entering the spring house on the flat gray rock, where buckets of milk and butter sat in transparent water. He found only sitting still to be unbearable. Knowing how much his teacher loved her pupils, he made the most intense efforts to copy her perfections. His earliest writing was full of scratchouts. "He has spared no pains," Suny said in praise, "to spell every word correctly."

Long before his mother permitted him to carry a gun, he followed his black-and-tan hound through the fields northwest of home. "A rabbit would jump up . . . that old pokey dog would strike the trail . . . and after a while he would catch that rabbit," Sawney recalled.

Up on the mountain field he flew his kite and felt the tug at his hand and the wind in his face. On a clear day he could see Chapel Hill. He found forests to roam, and could enter remote hollows where the deep shade dimmed the summer sun. He saw Nature angry and dangerous, too, flattening crops, rooting up trees, in winter numbing a body to the bone, and looking gray, brown, and dead. He enjoyed the strong taste of natural freedom.

At least once a vast cloud of passenger pigeons blackened the heavens, and Sawney remembered that chickens roosted in the daytime, the masses of wild birds made it so dark. The pigeons themselves, roosting at night in the forest, would pile high on top of each other and break large limbs from the trees; and men would strike out with big sticks and kill thousands, gathering up the beautiful birds the next morning for eating, or to boil them for packing away in lard. There were myriads of these small-brained birds. Could even this little boy, with his growing love of living things, imagine that within his lifetime, the last passenger pigeon would die in the Cincinnati Zoo?

He never lost his interest in things that move. An early tumble from a swing cut his chin severely. The painful accident left a permanent scar on the lower left side of his jaw. He was too stubborn, however, to let a memory make him afraid. His frame was no match for the intense spirit that welled up in his wide, blue eyes. He was always driving his frail body to do more.

"I never heard of work as a burden, but as a great privilege," he said. His first chores were feeding the pigs and lambs. Later, he learned to drive the team of oxen. But the first time he mounted a horse must have been his proudest moment. As he rode Old Jane on an errand one day, the horse fell on slippery ground, tossing Sawney. Ma and Sister Suny were frantic, but he treated the mishap with bravado. He had merely fallen into thick mud. He laughed at the sharp briars around Harmony Hill where he helped his Brother James to work the land. The hardest lesson was self-control.

The do-nothing Sabbath was his greatest problem. Doing nothing "to keep it holy" was impossible. One Sunday after church he jumped with his bare feet on two wide pots of juicy geraniums. The crunch was delicious, but the flowers were Grandmother Stanford's. When in dismay she called her grandson for a reckoning, he denied he had crushed the plants.

She looked at him sternly, "You are sure?"

"Yes ma'am, I'm sure."

Grandmother seized a little foot and planted it in a footprint on the soil of one of the pots. The fit was exact. She ordered the delinquent to bring her a switch from a peach tree.

"It shames me beyond expression," she said, "that a grandson of mine should tell a lie."

" 'Twasn't me that did it, Grandma; 'twas my foot that did it, not me."

"So," Grandmother said, peering over her spectacles. "Your foot did it, and not you. Far be it from me to punish an innocent boy. As *you* have done nothing wrong, my boy, I'll not switch you. But watch me switch this guilty foot!"

Sawney the Schoolmaster thought her lesson in integrity made sense: "Just so long as a child destroys, he is a savage." He told the story, quotations and all, to his eldest daughter Alla.

Fortunately, peach trees stand for pleasure more than they do for pain. Peaches were the little boy's favorite fruit. Before Grandmother died, Sawney proudly drove the Sunday wagon, taking the old lady to visit family back in Person County. She acquainted him with the "law of the road," allowing him to gather peaches from a farmer's tree to stuff his pockets, but no more, and directing him to plant the peachstones in a likely fence corner. Years later, he told his children, he was certain he ate fruit from the very trees he had planted.

His high spirits, however, continued to overflow into violence. He was the center of many a quarrel and fight with brothers, schoolmates, and slave children. His very spunk was a worry to his mother. He grew up fatherless in the arch-romantic South. People aped the social games they found on the pages of Sir Walter Scott. They memorized passages from his novels. They cultivated a beautiful courtesy toward the ladies. They also dueled and feuded and brawled and played with death.

"I've seen fifty fights in an afternoon at my little home community," Sawney told his students in later years. "One fellow would step out and draw a line and say, 'By gum, I can whip any man that toes the mark.' A fellow would toe the mark and they would go at it. How the blood in noses would fly." But the Widow Webb required her high-spirited son to face the ultimate consequences of rustic chivalry. "My mother took me to her knee and told me about some murders . . . and about the orphans and widows. I have never seen the day that I wouldn't suffer any insults on me that anybody could offer rather than take the husband away from the wife."

Whiskey was often the cause of high spirits and ugly tempers. All you could drink cost a nickel, exactly what Sister Suny charged for a day's tuition. In later years, Sawney recalled, "I was a little fellow and went up to the election. . . . They had whiskey to sell . . . drink all you wanted . . . then they would go out behind the barn to fight. I would go up on top of the barn so that the sticks and rocks wouldn't hit me. . . . I was reared in the sight of distilleries. There was no restriction. . . . I have seen hundreds of my neighbors drunk at a time. There were temperance societies and a great many people took temperance pledges. There were a great many sober people who never touched it."

Sawney's mother taught him that he must not touch it. "My son," she used to say, "if you don't learn to control your temper, you will end on the gallows." The little boy fought an inner battle early.

He also learned to make creative mischief out of boyish hate. He knew that good people like Ma and Suny were thin from working hard and eating wisely. Uncle Saurin, who liked loads of pepper in his sausage, was fat, with triple chins. Uncle Saurin detested guineas and their raucous cries. Sawney vowed that guineas were the pleasantest, most musical fowls imaginable, and he would have guineas forever around his place, just for their style.

One sultry, breezeless summer afternoon Sawney and his brother Tip heard only two sounds: the cooing of mourning doves, and the hoarse rising and falling of snores from a visiting carriage. The vehicle had springs of extra strength, and stood in the driveway, shafts aground. The frail little boy with the wideset eyes and up-turned nose crept up and looked in. Yes, Uncle Saurin was sleeping soundly, bulk overflowing. His mouth was open. He roared and snorted. Fattest man in the world, Sawney supposed. How fat?

Sawney nudged Brother Tip just behind him, and drew a knife and string out of his pocket. He carefully measured the distance of the depressed springs from top to bottom. Then he cut the string to that exact length with his knife. The boys stifled their laughter, and tiptoed away. Some time later, Uncle Saurin climbed ponderously out of his carriage and waddled into the house. The boys left their game of marbles. They gathered the largest stones they could handle. They brought them to the carriage, piled them on the floor, and measured the springs, adding to the rockpile above them until the pressure exactly matched Uncle Saurin's weight. Finally they moved the pile to the farm scales and weighed it in.

That night at supper, they could hardly wait until Uncle Saurin had asked the blessing and Ma had filled her brother's plate with his favorite sausage.

"Uncle Saurin, how much do you weigh?" Tip asked.

"That is none of your business," Uncle Saurin replied.

"Please, Uncle Saurin, tell us," Sawney said.

"My weight is my own affair," Uncle said, and went on eating.

The two boys then looked at each other and announced in unison: "Uncle Saurin weighs 322 pounds."

After they explained their prank, the fat man sputtered and turned purple, while Mother Webb tried to look stern: "Boys, I am ashamed and distressed that you should treat Uncle Saurin with such little consideration." But it was a boy's progress, a triumph of nonviolent mischief, a story a father would tell on himself to eight grown sons and daughters.

Mother began sending Sawney alone on horseback the ten miles to Haw River, to have the corn ground into meal. At first, it seemed a long, long way. Then the advent of the stagecoach began to make this local travel very tame. The stage arrived at Oaks with a clatter, wheels spinning, Sawney's hero sitting high in his beautiful leather boots and broad-brimmed hat. Driver and vehicle were the medium supreme, bringing news and mail and glimpses of the outer world, and sometimes a visitor from afar. Neighbors gathered around the driver. Grown men talked politics with him. Girls admired him. Half-grown boys envied him.

"A psychologist would have relegated me to a livery stable about the time I was in my teens. . . . It was my highest ambition to drive a stagecoach. Fortunately, my mother saw better," Sawney said. His father had seen better, too. Sawney was already part of the Bingham school community, and now he was entering its doors as a student. It was 1856. He was nearly fourteen years of age, all ready for his college preparation. But why was it that everywhere he went he seemed to be the smallest and the frailest? His arrival as a "newie" in the schoolyard brought him instant torture.

III. He Thrashed a Boy, Looking Nice and Sweet

Books are much dearer
than any living friends.
From them we never apprehend
any harsh words
or any unkind look.
They are the most pleasant companions
in the world.
—SAWNEY WEBB

No sooner did Sawney enter Bingham schoolyard than a bully named Calvin began to pull him around by the hair, twist his fingers, and do everything else he could think of to torment the smaller boy. "It would just tickle him to death," Sawney said. "I was absolutely helpless. I would run from him but he could outrun me." Among the great poplars, oaks, and hickories, he lost every game of hide and seek he tried to play. "He weighed twice as much as I did, he sat foot in his classes, he never knew anything." Sawney called Calvin's bullying "the great torture of my life." Boys who knew him decades later as a schoolmaster found it hard to imagine him as the victim.

"One morning we were all out under a big poplar tree. . . . Calvin was putting me through the usual rounds. A crowd of boys were

standing around and looking on and laughing." Newie Webb noticed another boy about Calvin's size walk up. "He didn't cuss.
. . . He just walked up and said, 'Calvin, I have stood this as long as I can stand it. You take every opportunity to bully this little boy. Hereafter I will take it as a personal matter.' He turned around and walked off, studying his lesson. . . . I was just as safe from then on as if I were encased in armor. Calvin never pulled my hair. He was just as polite to me as he could be. I made a great fool of myself by not going to the teacher and telling him about the bullying."

The teacher in charge, William James Bingham, described his government as "kindly and parental but firm . . . regarding himself as standing in the relation of parent to every pupil." No one withstood the flash of this small wiry Irishman's dark eye. "When his foot hits the pavement, dong will go the clock," old boys correctly told the new. Old Bingham was precisely on time when he stepped onto the piazza of his log schoolhouse.

Little Sawney read his first Latin sentence, *Tempus fugit*, "time flies." He began memorizing Old Stoddard's *Latin Grammar*. Assignments were not long but they had to be learned perfectly. In class Old Bingham never used a book. He sat up and made goose quill pens while the boys recited. He pointed his finger at a boy and asked for the genitive form of *tempus*.

"*Tempe*," said the boy.

"Next," snapped Old Bingham.

"*Tempo*," said another boy.

"Next! Next! Next!" Answers must come instantly—*tempus fugit*. Seven boys wrong in all.

Then "*temporis*" from a boy who had done his work.

"Right," Old Bingham said. "You seven boys come here." He stung their seven behinds with the touch of hickory. This teacher communicated belief and expectations.

"His theory was that the boy knew," Sawney said. "When a boy missed declining a word, he thrashed him. . . . He wasn't mad. He thrashed a boy, all the time looking nice and sweet like he was doing the nicest job he ever did in his life. I would watch the old man sitting back and smiling like he was eating peaches or Georgia watermelons. I never heard him stand and lecture boys. . . . That's the only school I ever saw where thirty or forty boys knew their lessons every day, never missed." Old Bingham never believed a dispassionate switching was harmful to a growing personality. He was, however, certain that unrestricted use of pocket money was "everywhere, and to all boys injurious, to many, ruinous," and he said so in his one-page sixteen-point circular.

The Select School of W. J. Bingham and Sons aimed "to make *good scholars* and *good men*" so that "no profane or vicious boy, no confirmed idler, in a word, no boy who does *no good,* or who *does others harm,*" was welcome. Deportment and academic progress were "truly reported at the end of each session," twenty weeks long. As Sawney's brother Tip bitterly learned, Old Bingham never flattered. The school was expensive for its times: $125 in gold per session in advance, for board, bedding, fuel and washing, as well as for tuition, which alone amounted to about $75. In that era of wild-cat banking Old Bingham accepted no paper money although he was roundly criticized for persisting in this policy. Moreover, enrollment was tantamount to indebtedness unless "an act of God" kept a boy away.

Parents all over the South accepted the stern conditions, and so did many—but not all—of their sons. While Bingham was teaching in the county-seat town of Hillsboro, complaints had been especially bitter. One boy wrote his father:

We have had to go to our prayers at nine o'clock and get up before sunrise and go to our books. The boys are much displeased with Mr. Bingham's laws . he won't allow them to go down town without his permission nor to any where else [.] he makes us get a bible lesson every sunday to say monday morning and if we don't know every word of it he will put them up stairs and keep them from their dinner. . . . Mr. Bingham has lost nine schollars [*sic*] and from all accounts, he will loose [*sic*] a great many more.

Bingham School managed to survive the "loosing" of "schollars" for almost another century, until a disastrous fire, combined with the great financial crash, ended its life in 1929.

W. J. Bingham's father, an Irish revolutionary who fled to America, had founded the portable family school in eastern North Carolina as early as 1793. The Bingham circular of the 1850s said little of the Oaks environment except that boys were required to go to church on Sunday and not make accounts at business houses. However, students had the run of God's great gymnasium in their free hours and they engaged in a variety of vigorous enterprises: hunting, fishing, trapping, and games, including shinny, a rustic version of field hockey. Bingham's was an outdoor school.

Young Sawney was absorbing the schoolmaker's art, as he consciously was learning how to learn. He always found memorizing hard but he did it best in the morning. He mastered Latin and Greek grammars "before breakfast." In the schoolhouse, the one Greek dictionary lay on a table with its back nailed down. When a boy wanted to know a Greek word that dictionary gave him the definition only in Latin. Equipment was as rude as at Sister Suny's. Sawney never saw a school bench with a back on it until after he was grown.

Brilliant William Bingham, the older son, was the most interesting conversationalist Sawney would ever meet. In a few years he would begin writing his own textbooks, and the students believed he actually thought in Latin. When he told a delinquent scholar, "*Veni ad lignum*" [come to the wood], the class knew the boy faced a switching—not on the buttocks, however, but on the hands. Sawney never "came to the wood" but when he began to read Virgil, he graduated from study by candlelight. "I bought a little glass lamp, paid five dollars for it and two dollars for a gallon of red coal oil— I didn't think a king had anything finer." During the slack season or when he was ailing, he would go Saturdays to the hayloft to read by himself—away from idle boarders, younger children, everyone.

A favorite story of his gave lively shapes to his youthful dreams. A young student falls in love with a beautiful maiden isolated in a ruined tower, rescues her from the unbridled lust of a corrupt nobleman, saves her unjustly accused father from being burned at the stake, and cares for them as his wife and his father-in-law forever after. "I remember the charm of that morning, and it will go with me forever," Sawney said of the morning he read "The Student of Salamanca" from the pages of Irving's *Bracebridge Hall*.

One subject he learned to detest was English grammar. "I 'parsed' and 'diagrammed' in my day," he remembered ruefully. His own school of the future never imposed an English grammar on any boy.

A Bingham policy that stirred his youthful sense of justice was the choice of commencement speakers. "As a boy I said it wa'n't fair. . . . It isn't fair! . . . They picked out a few of the big boys and let them speak at commencement and excluded the rest of us." Every boy in school should have the chance to speak if he wants to! Oratory was the masculine fine art, the supreme extracurricular activity. The shy little boy, who did not want to remain shy, found it disheartening to be denied his chance on the platform. He envied the Big Men on Bingham Campus, the Public Debaters.

Responsibilities kept him furiously busy at home. As older brothers grew up and married, or went to college, young Sawney took charge of the farm for his mother's sake. He studied hard at school, he did heavy work like plowing during holidays, he even became her deputy in the fields.

"My health gave out. The survival of the fittest didn't look like it was coming my way." He was ailing as he began his sophomore year. By the following May he apparently reached a state of exhaustion. As he struggled out of bed, the measles struck. "He has not given up as much as any of the others," his mother wrote, but by early June he was "quite sick."

He had to quit school. By mid-November he was rallying, and at last resumed his strenuous routine. In time, he was proud to say, he grew strong enough to win a footrace at the Orange County Fair. Physically, he was a late bloomer—frail, small, and intensely serious. His face was owl-like in its solemnity.

His Cousin Shap, who came to board at Stony Point, was vastly different: "I hailed from the metropolitan and wide open village of Memphis, Tennessee, which I then thought was the largest and most magnificent city in the world," Shap recalled. "I thought I had all the education there was, and was going to Bingham's to pick up any 'dropped stitches' that might be needed to fit me for taking charge of the University and waking the old thing up."

Then Old Bingham examined him. "Young man," the schoolmaster said bluntly, "your elementary education has been sadly neglected; you are assigned to the Freshman class." Shap was reduced to a seat among the "infants." "All my cock-a-doodle-do vanished. I was homesick," said Cousin Shap, but two relatives gave him their sympathy. "Aunt Adeline and Sawney . . . encouraged me with assurances that I would soon make it up and go into a higher class." Shap did make it up and after a year went on to Chapel Hill, but the two cousins had formed a lifetime friendship.

Sawney also found a lifetime friend in his teacher Robert Bingham. In 1857, this younger of the two Bingham sons returned to Oaks as a first-honors graduate of the state university. The self-confident, articulate young man taught Sawney most of his classes.

The pupil began to look toward the law. He dreamed of states-

manship. His memory clung to eminent examples. His own grandfather, Richard Stanford, had been a congressman. Sawney persuaded his mother to let him go see President Buchanan in a
neighboring town and he tasted the thrill of being personally introduced to the chief executive.

"I used to wonder what sort of a man Henry Clay was," Sawney
said. He envied those who had seen the Great Compromiser and
asked them about him. Why, Henry Clay spoke to thousands at
once. He would look at five acres of people, and raise his voice, and
the throngs could hear his every word! Sawney's family, heroes,
teachers—all were ardent Whig believers in the national Union.
However, there was growing division in the nation. In 1859, the
youth saw and heard President Buchanan again, under grim circumstances, although it was Brother Richard's commencement at
the university.

The president warned the large Chapel Hill crowd that the
Union was alarmingly close to breaking up: "Let . . . the members
of this Union separate; let thirty Republics rise up against each
other, and it would be the most fatal day for the liberties of the
human race that ever dawned upon any land." Sawney knew about
the Abolitionists. He was reading more and more about Secession-
ists. What future was there for W. R. Webb, the young Unionist
Whig?

Studies, farm work, and family troubles preoccupied his mind.
His disturbed, gaunt eldest sister Henrietta had been in and out of
the asylum at Raleigh. Brother Tip had quit Bingham's in anger
after Mr. Bingham wrote his mother that the boy was doing no
good in his studies. The widow's migraine headaches grew worse.

Then terrible news came, and Sawney had to deliver it personally to Cousin Shap. In February of 1860 the newspapers were full
of it: James L. Webb was shot to death on a Memphis street just
outside his office. Shap's father had died instantly. Sawney hurried
over to offer Shap the sympathy of the family and help him get
ready for the long journey home. Sawney was in a saddle fast, galloping along the ten-mile dirt road to the university. When he located Shap, however, he realized that Shap knew nothing. How
does one say, "Your father is dead," to a boy who has grown up
having a father? Sawney, somehow, broke the grievous news. Shap
could not believe it. He went off to Raleigh to telegraph home. Im-

mediately, however, he found the Memphis slaying a big story in all the capital newspapers.

Uncle James's business partner had been security for a deputy sheriff. Recently the partner had informed the county court that the deputy was collecting money under false pretenses and was seen hanging around gambling rooms and saloons. The deputy had blamed Uncle James for the partner's report. A crooked law man, hanging around saloons and gambling dens, had caused this violent death on city cobblestones.

Just a few months before, an angry northern idealist in the name of God had led a biracial force against the U.S. Arsenal at Harper's Ferry. Exactly two months before Uncle James was slain, this same idealist, John Brown, had himself been hanged for his miniature insurrection. Suspicion and hatred and anger and violence seemed epidemic.

On a visit to Chapel Hill, Sawney wandered out where students were buried. "I walked into the cemetery and there was a column—plain marble, just broken off. The thoughts that came to me have never left me. . . . A young life broken off at the beginning."

Sawney had scored firsts in most of his subjects. His deportment at Bingham's was "uniformly that of a gentleman." He was a member of a social club. He had good friends. But . . . *a young life broken off at the beginning. . . .*

In a Spencerian hand with very few neat corrections, he wrote one of his last essays at Bingham's. In two years he would never write neatly again:

The wisdom of Providence nowhere manifests itself more plainly than in throwing, as it were, a veil over the future. Could man . . . see himself reared to any exalted station, lauded and held in admiration by all the world . . . his life would be one continual scene of unpleasant excitement. And, on the other hand, could he know that his whole life would be one of adversity . . . deprived of everything that would gladden his heart, that man's life would be an insupportable burden.

After a few uncertain months at the university, he would face prolonged adversity—"four years of war and five years of reconstruction taken out of the heart of my young life."

He felt a sense of accomplishment at graduation and enjoyed a "splendiferous" senior party. Very soon, however, it was July. "I went down to Chapel Hill with a feeling of more terror and fear than when I went into battle," he confessed to his own students many years later.

At Bingham's a lone bully had tortured him. Young men organized bullying into hazing where he was headed now. It was not enough for rowdy students to fill classrooms with junk and place cows in the college chapel. "People would see around a hotel a lot of loud-mouthed bums that made faces at strangers, that hazed every freshman that drove up in a stage," Sawney said.

The homesick youth with the scared look climbed down from the coach, handled his luggage as best he could, and between rock walls entered the grove-like campus—the smallest boy as far as he could see. The largest he could see—a huge, broad-faced fellow—made straight for him. Sawney remembered, "I took it for granted that here was the Goliath of the Sophomores and he is come out to bedevil me."

"Nicholson," the big stranger introduced himself.

Sawney measured him, and thought: "He can whip me and a dozen more like me."

"Are you a member of the Church?" Nicholson asked.

Sawney admitted to being a Methodist.

"So am I," Nicholson replied, "and we are going to have a YMCA meeting before daylight."

Next morning, Sawney found more than a hundred boys in a candlelit room for prayer and comradeship. "Ed Nicholson was there . . . and he put his great brawny arm around me and I have loved his memory ever since." There was a short future ahead for Ed Nicholson.

Immediate problems diverted the mind from weightier anxieties. The price of one textbook staggered Sawney: Keener's *Greek Grammar*, two volumes, $18.00 plus $1.50 for the binding. He wrote his mother, and she wrote him right back to buy it. "While many wealthy men drew a line on buying such extravagant textbooks, I had the best."

Among the teachers, Sawney most admired Fatty Phillips. All his life, he said that for him, the Reverend Charles Phillips *was* the university. Head massive, face leonine, gait gouty, coat short, expression good-natured, heart as big as a water bucket, brain as big as his paunch—that was Old Fatty as colleagues, students, and university historians remembered him. He was so talented in mathematics that colleagues felt it was a pity he refused to specialize. But Professor Phillips was too involved. He preached, studied theology and political economy. He zealously enforced university discipline and sometimes lost popularity in doing so. He arose from a hasty dinner to take classes on field trips in surveying. He seldom thought of his health. Phillips's belief in shooting intellectually above the students' heads was distressing to some. He insisted it aroused young men to "higher things."

Freshman Webb adhered to Chapel Hill's honor system. He took an active part in the debating society. He joined the DKE fraternity, but he found the violence of social life disturbing. Students took turns providing candles and firewood for their rooms. Once, partners could not agree whose turn came next. The word "liar" passed between them, a "duel" followed, and both died of gunshots. Sawney remembered this incident all his life. "Suppose I had been challenged," he thought. "I would have been branded as a coward if I hadn't accepted. . . . I thought it out . . . I never believed there was a man on this earth that could wheel and fire quicker." Sawney's quickness would save his life in battle. But he always referred to duelling as that "field of *dis*honor" when as a teacher he talked of the sanctity of human life.

Riotous neighbors forced the youth to change his room after the Christmas holidays. The death of one of them in February stunned the campus community and Sawney wrote a somber letter home:

The faculty last session requested his guardian not to return him, that he was killing himself drinking and injuring others. Reports say that after the end of last session, he quit drinking and became a real clever, sober fellow. His friends didn't wish him to return to the Hill, but he insisted he should come on a visit. He came, got with his old crowd & drank to excess. He went to his room—and an hour or so afterwards was found in the last agonies of death.

Friends found "an emptied vial, labelled 'laudanum' . . . to counteract the influence of the liquor." The young man apparently took an overdose. Another young life broken off at the beginning. . . .

College life for young Sawney was never without undercurrents of serious emergency. In October, an old Bingham schoolmate had written a prophetic letter from Oxford, Georgia, where he was attending Emory College: "Sawney, if you were to see the companies that are forming all over the state & hear the people down here talk, you would think that *war* was coming sure enough." The writer was sure that if Lincoln were elected, "South Carolina will be as good as her word to secede, Lincoln's duty is then to whip her back which will inevitably bring bloodshed & Civil War."

Ed Nicholson had written even more disturbing news at Christmastime:

I had entertained a strong hope (I still hope) for a compromise. . . . But now my hopes have, indeed, grown faint, occasioned by the news which my father brought me from the south. He has been spending the winter in Miss[issippi]. Oh! if you could hear him talk you would be a stronger Union man than ever. He says that one of the largest slave holders in Miss[issippi], was threatened with a "tar & feathering" for simply expressing a conservative sentiment.

Sawney's old chief justice friend, Thomas Ruffin of Haw River, opposed secession, and successfully urged compromise or concession or conciliation—anything to prevent war and save the Union. Ruffin joined four other North Carolinians at a Washington Peace Conference. The five statesmen soon returned, however, with the feeling that they had been rebuffed. After the firing on Fort Sumter in April of 1861, the new president wired Governor John W. Ellis to send two regiments of North Carolina men to the Federal Army.

Sawney was aghast. "I didn't believe it was justifiable. For my life, I can't see that if Mr. Lincoln had met with Mr. Davis as Davis requested and gone over their troubles with commissioners from both sides, they couldn't have come to a peaceful settlement. . . . I never had been a secessionist. . . . All my neighbors and kinfolks were for the Union." Sawney confided in Sister Addie that he wept "bitter tears" over his dilemma. "But Mr. Lincoln said, 'I want 75,000 troops' in response to Mr. Davis' request for peace. Here, you—Tennessee, North Carolina, and Virginia—must furnish your part of the troops to subdue the South. We *were* the South!"

In April Chapel Hill became a festival of azaleas, wood iris, trillium, redbud, white dogwood, and scented plum. The oaks, elms, and tulip poplars were green again. In April four student companies began drilling for war. In response to Lincoln's call for troops, Governor Ellis sent thousands of volunteers and a shipment of muskets to the other side. Old Judge Ruffin raised his arms above his head and shouted, "I say fight! fight! fight!"

"All my college mates were hurried out to battle," Sawney said. Students began leaving at the rate of eight to ten a day. "Mr. Lincoln's haste," Sawney always insisted, "doubled the Confederacy and doubled the enemy he had to defeat."

College boy Webb volunteered. He joined the infantry company in Judge Ruffin's County of Alamance, whose eastern boundary now contained his home. The Widow Webb was "sick, very sick" in her bed that week in mid-June her soldier boy of Company H marched hurriedly away toward the North.

It had been goodbye, indeed, to young Ed Nicholson. The first time soldier Ed came within reach of a Federal battery, Sawney's good-natured, loyal big friend had his head blown off.

IV. A Dog's Life—
and I Was Scared

My son, I tried war—
I tried it as a private,
as a non-commissioned officer,
and it is a dog's life.
I started out from college
with brass bands playing . . .
and like young David,
I was going with my slingshot
to kill Goliath
without a bit of trouble.
—SAWNEY WEBB

Donning gray, doing drill, eating barbecue, watching drunk comrades, warming to young ladies' glances, bidding romantic goodbyes, mustering with the Fifteenth Regiment, rushing north to Yorktown, but arriving too late for the first fight—how deceptive the round of fleeting excitements had been! To Sawney it seemed that "for fifty-two solid weeks we dug and dug and dug, and our hands were sore . . . and we had to do what the officers told us, and I realized that the life of a soldier might be attractive, but it was a dog's life."

At the age of eighteen, he was beginning a brutal four-year course in human nature. "There were fellows there from way back up in the mountains away from schools and civilization. . . . They had all curious sorts of superstitions," he recalled. Early one morning Sawney entered a cabin with a gun on his shoulder. A giant of a hillbilly tumbled out of his bunk, bounded up, and said angrily: "Didn't you know that if a fellow comes into this cabin with a gun on his shoulder before breakfast, somebody will have to die before night?" Sawney did not know, but he would try to be tactful.

He was promoted to first orderly sergeant, and had his daguerreotype taken—a handsome well-knit fellow with a mane of wavy hair, and ornamental stripes on his sleeves. His new job was unenviable—he issued rations. "I was a beardless boy who weighed just 108 pounds. Sometimes they would give us a piece of beef that five men could have eaten and I would have to divide it among a hundred men," Sawney remembered. "These diplomats would try to bribe me. . . . Oh, it was a hard place! I prayed God every day to make me just.". . . He managed to win their regard. "Those fellows . . . used to come to me to write their letters for them . . . the biggest compliment I ever had."

A deepening conviction put Sawney into more serious difficulty. He refused to issue whiskey rations in the face of final orders from the Colonel himself: "I told him . . . that if it was necessary for me to do so, I would prefer being reduced in the ranks." Sawney always expressed pride in the upshot: unanimous election to a higher place.

He swam off some of his homesickness in the rolling James River. He exulted in the big victory at Manassas of the southern War for Independence, and hoped "the northerners . . . will let us alone."

Then in the humid heat diseases spread. Camp life among the swamps was too much for Tarheels from the foothills and the mountains. Sawney tended the sick. He watched men die. On August 1, he was sick himself, along with eighty per cent of the regiment. Thom Morrow's "servant," Black Thom, nursed him and many other soldiers. Shaking and burning uncontrollably, Sawney was finally shipped up near Warwick Courthouse. It was malaria. "I was in the hands of ignorant people without a doctor. Not a drop of water was allowed me for days & days. Under the torture and the *un*reason . . . I planned a home right by a freestone spring. . . . I thought sincerely that I would stay there and drink that cool water to the end of my life," he wrote. Death and disability cost the regiment over fifteen per cent of its men. Survivors renewed their "dog's life" in October.

"Cousin Sawney," wrote a well-meaning girl, "it is the greatest desire of my heart that our friends may return to us, crowned with laurels of immortal fame. . . ." Cousin Sawney's "laurels" were recurring chills and fever, sore hands—and later in 1861, sore feet he severely bruised on the rocks where he was working. He resolved to resist disease by bathing every day the seasons around—even when he had to walk a mile and break ice in a stream.

He also vowed to complete his formal education. He asked his sisters to return his letters with corrected errors. He read all the books he could find half a dozen times. He made a collection—a Roman history, a Bible, Milton's poems, a Greek mythology. Sawney recalled, "I was sitting out under a tree and an ignorant man came out and said, 'Why do you sit here and read all the time?' I said, 'I am trying to read history.' He said, 'We are making history.' I said, 'Yes, but we haven't been reading it.' "

As the New Year of 1862 began, Black Thom himself became critically ill. In his gratitude, Sawney nursed the slave, waited on him, and marveled at his patient endurance under affliction. At times, the sick man was delirious, at other times he talked feelingly of his wife and children. Often Sawney heard him pleading with his Maker to take him to his "long home." "I asked him if he thought he would get well," Sawney remembered. "He said 'No.' I then asked if he wanted to go home. His reply was, 'This world is not my home.' " Not long after this gentle irony, Black Thom quietly died. The "noble-hearted" Thom's example loosened the scales of caste and race that limited the nineteen-year-old southern soldier's vision. Sawney wrote in groping, college-boy rhetoric:

Would to heaven all the earth would travel his way; if so, how soon the hellish deeds daily enacted in this unnatural and cruel war would be done away with, and all the world would live in peace. . . . The Goddess of Discord . . . could no more stir up strife among the family of nations . . . no more could many complain that while languishing upon a bed of disease, no hand ministered to his wants, and while parched with fever he found no kind sympathetic friend. Black Thom wouldn't hesitate to spend the last six-pence he had for comfortables for any of us when we were sick, and if necessary sit by our beds . . . to comply with any of our wants.

Winter brought sleet and snow and freezing rain. Once Sawney awoke with a stream pouring through his blankets. He was debating re-enlistment in February. Then the Confederate Congress passed the controversial Conscription Acts of 1862, and the army canceled promised re-enlistment furloughs home. Sawney joined in the furious resentment, declaring that the government had broken faith. However, he went on obeying orders, and in the spring, the big emergency came. The Yankees were threatening Richmond, the Confederate capital, from the peninsula and also from the sea.

The Fifteenth North Carolina took a position at Lee's Mill between Yorktown and the James. Yankee field guns opened up on the dam site. The youth no longer had time for books. He studied men. He noticed that the big talkers and fire eaters bolted from danger, and the quiet pale fellows stood firm. The colonel in command was among twelve regimental dead. Military elections on May 3 resulted in an almost complete change of officers. One Confederate army evacuated Yorktown, and began moving the defense line back. Sawney's regiment was among the last to withdraw.

Spring rains turned the roads into a miry nightmare. "I remember when it was pouring down rain and we had not one board of shelter. I felt that I couldn't survive the night. I didn't believe any human being could live. Some soldier way down in the camp began to sing a song. He closed with 'So let the world wag as it will, / I will be gay and happy still.' And the third time ten thousand voices rang in the chorus. I felt like I could stand all the rain and mud and whip four Yankees besides."

They slogged on without food, carrying their hundred pounds on their backs. A promise went down the dripping, exhausted line that only a few miles ahead they would eat at last. Sawney remembered, "When I got to the courthouse, they gave me a double handful of corn . . . in the shape you feed it to cattle." Footsore, heartsick, tired, wet, and resentful, Sawney began to grind the parched corn between his teeth. "I was complaining. I looked around and saw an old fellow pounding corn between two rocks. He looked up and said, 'I had all my teeth shot out in the Mexican War.'" Sawney gritted his teeth and chewed hard.

When June arrived the regiment formed a battleline at Fair Oaks and learned that Robert E. Lee was now supreme commander. They remained under daily fire from Federal batteries, but morale, under Lee, began to rise.

Sawney almost lost his life trying to see another general. "I was in front of a large crowd. . . . When he came in sight that man had on a little bit of a cap that I could buy for a dime. . . . He had on a plain suit. He rode on an old horse. That man was Stonewall Jackson. . . . Twenty thousand men rushed pell mell, just to see Stonewall Jackson. All the officers in the world couldn't have kept those men from breaking ranks." It stuck in Sawney's mind that Stonewall Jackson had once been a poor schoolteacher.

In late June the regiment began scrambling over deserted earthworks and sweeping around the head of White Oak Swamp, a vast tangle of dark bushes and evil-smelling water. Cautious McClellan was withdrawing the Federal invaders. At Malvern Hill he decided to make a stand. The top commanded a view of grainfields running into woods and lowlands, where the advancing Confederates began to gather. It was July 1, 1862. Sawney's regiment moved forward to support southern batteries on the edge of woods about a thousand yards from the Yankee line. A horrible concentration of Federal shells soon silenced every Confederate gun.

Then the incredible command came from brigade headquarters: "General Cobb told our men that he wanted us to take a battery . . . on the hill, about a hundred guns," remembered Sawney. In between were not only open fields, but the well-fortified Federal infantry lines. "Some fellows said they were not afraid any more than if they were going to eat breakfast. They were cowards."

The company took orders to fix bayonets. Sawney was "scared." It was a bright blazing day. He ran forward. The bullets began to sing around him. Through a cornfield on a rise, Sawney continued to run. He was hit. He continued, faltering. He was hit again. As he fell, a bullet grazed his back with the sharpest pain he would ever feel.

He lay between the rows of corn. His right shoulder came alive with aching. He found his right arm useless and bleeding. With his left hand, he tried to dig. Screams and shrieks of physical agony on the hillside in the blazing heat mingled with the cannon roars and gunfire. The charge had failed. "As I lay there wounded I was still scared," he recalled.

Sawney felt he was literally drying up—"[I was] so thirsty that my mind seemed to be going from me and my tongue swollen till it almost filled my mouth." Someone crept out and gave him water to drink. His Good Samaritan was a Catholic priest. He remembered lying on Malvern Hill from Tuesday to Friday, after humidity had turned to rain, and the red soil had turned to mud. McClellan had gone on withdrawing, and the Federals no longer threatened. Yet the wounded were more than the small Confederate medical corps could handle immediately. Seventy per cent of Sawney's company alone were casualties. He waited on a hill of mass murder, crawling with the agonies of the living.

A surgeon finally reached him, found the shoulder wound dangerously close to a major artery, reached with a long sharpened fingernail into the flesh, and extracted the bullet. Nerves had already been severed. There was no feeling in his arm and hand. There would always be pain and throbbing in his shoulder. A wagon ride to Richmond—and he was in the hospital, tossing, unable to sleep. One night he rested gloriously. On awaking, he found his head under the touch of a soft hand. A beautiful girl was comforting him, almost like a dream. When he woke up again, she was gone. Sawney was home by late July, with his mother, his sisters and his younger brothers. He did what farm tasks he could.

At the end of 1862, James H. Horner offered him a position in his man-short Classical School at Oxford. For teaching a couple of classes and giving military drill, he would receive at least $200 for five months, and maybe more. The town was not too far away from Oaks. On January 16, 1863, he made his teaching debut, teaching boys in a Latin grammar class.

He wrote Suny, "Though they committed to memory very well, they didn't seem to have the remotest idea that what they repeated had any meaning whatever. I found it very difficult to make them understand the simplest things, owing I guess to the pernicious effects of bad teaching." He taught on into February. He confessed, "I like teaching better than I thought I would, though there is not much fun in it."

Dr. Strudwick at Hillsboro had Sawney's furlough extended: "He partly closes his hand but has no power to open it—nor can he elevate the hand or wrist. . . . Mr. Webb is therefore utterly unfit for duty." He was the choice of his company, however, for the post of first lieutenant. By March he was again in military service, among sandflies, mosquitoes, chills and alligators, down on the Coosawhatchie River, between Charleston and Savannah. He passed his lieutenancy examinations. He learned to eat grits. He tried to appreciate cypress country and the graceful Spanish moss. He complained of not receiving letters from the fair sex, yet admitted he had himself to blame. He was miserable. "My hand is much improved, as I can drill an hour, but I can't march more than three miles." The weight of a pack on his shoulder caused him virtually to collapse from pain. By late May he knew he could not remain with his regiment. Young Sawney looked forward to eating peaches at home.

Before discharge, however, he passively took part in "the most awful scene I have ever beheld." His regiment formed three sides of a square, to watch on the fourth side a violent drama unfold: A deserter sitting on his coffin, the adjutant reading charges and the finding of the court, a minister solemnly speaking, the doomed man briefly kneeling by his coffin, the command to fire given, only one ball penetrating his body, the reserve squad marching up and missing him, then the "poor man" dying in agony at last from the first bullet's gradual effects. Sawney pitied the man, the man's wife, and their little child. His reason told him—tragically—that a deserter must be executed. A deserter endangered the nation. This was war.

In mid-summer of 1863, Meade's Federals were sending Lee's army reeling south from Gettysburg, and a general out west named U. S. Grant took possession of Vicksburg, the last Confederate stronghold on the strategic Mississippi River. Southern soldiers plundered their own people. William Bingham went deserter-hunting at home. Brother John himself stood guard duty at Oaks with a rusty musket as Bingham's became a military school.

Sawney himself was now at Chapel Hill, a disabled veteran at twenty, with one desperate hope for a livelihood. For a time he walked the campus in Brother Dick's old coat that hung about his scrawny body like a robe. A weather vane was throbbing in his shoulder.

A riot in nearby Raleigh blew the top off his indignation. "That Georgians should presume to suppress treason in N. C.! It is an insult to our authorities . . . there is no end to crimes of violence when mob law is allowed to prevail." Deep South troops had wrecked the press of a newspaper that was already calling for surrender. The War for Southern Independence looked more and more like a lost cause.

Studying seemed to be a lost cause too. Sawney's memory was quite treacherous. He had forgotten so much Greek that he seriously considered using a translation, but abandoned the idea on grounds it would ruin his scholarship; ". . . since I will be entirely dependent on that as a support, it becomes me to do everything in my power to improve it & nothing to injure it," Sawney wrote. Mathematics gave him extreme difficulty, but Greek came easier. Taking great pains, he reviewed.

The family's top scholar was at home. Brother John scored first in every subject at Bingham's but arithmetic, and the "passable" he received in that course made him weep with shame. In the house John was seldom without a book, but he also worked hard and regularly on the farm. Shortages everywhere were serious. Once the family admitted they did not have a horse healthy enough to bring Sawney home the ten miles from Chapel Hill.

Ex-lieutenant Webb spent hours in his second-story room on the northwest corner of Old South. From his front window he could see the Old Well, the Davie Poplar, and the village beyond, but the campus was a ghost of its former self. He wrote home for goose quill pens to spare him pain. "I find it much easier to work with them." One desolate night he sat down in his room and read Cicero's Latin essay on friendship. Every thought seemed to underscore the tragedy abroad: "Friendship can exist only between good men. . . . If you eliminate from nature the tie of love, there will be an end of house and city, nor will so much as the cultivation of the soil be left. The underhandedness of the cunning and the sly is what we have earnestly to guard against. . . ."

At the end of the session, Sawney ranked as the best scholar in the sophomore class. Schoolmaster Horner offered him $1,250 this time for five months. Old W. J. Bingham wanted Sawney too. The young man went home to be with his family.

Twelve days after Lincoln gave U. S. Grant the authority to end the war, Sawney was Private Webb again. He could not march, but he could ride with Company K in the Second North Carolina Cavalry. His life that spring of 1864 became galloping raid, attack and fight, withdraw and raid again, with few hours' sleep in a rain-drenched uniform. "I have broken down two horses in the last month," he wrote in May. For days in a squad, he skirmished with small numbers of the enemy to learn later that they had been part of some of the greatest battles: Spottsylvania Courthouse, for instance, and Yellow Tavern, where Jeb Stuart died.

Sawney traveled once-beautiful country that was now barren, the people having lost their substance, their very all. He bitterly reported the vindictiveness of some white Federal officers: "The Negroes are made spokesmen to humiliate the citizens. Any order from them, however arbitrary or unreasonable, if not immediately complied with, the offender is ruthlessly shot. . . . A widow lady . . . gave me numerous instances of this kind. . . . We are depressed when we find our patriotic people suffering such outrages & we are not able to defend them." Sawney also saw a few Negroes taken prisoner being rushed off into the woods to an obvious fate by Rebel soldiers. The nasty brutishness of war hatred left no dignity to either side, to either race. Paranoid nightmares took away reason and undoubtedly a great deal of the truth. Brother Dick, an Army chaplain, wrote sadly: "This is a demoralizing kind of life, so hardening to human feelings. I can now walk over a battlefield and see the ground strewn with dead bodies, or see a man's lim[b] amputated without any of the tendency of fainting the sight of blood used to cause."

Sawney's health was precarious and poor. Back on the lines starving, he watched Yankees hold up fresh meat with taunts and jeers. He willingly joined in a gallop that fall, far behind the Yankee lines in a mad grab for enemy beef on the hoof. Sawney was one of Wade Hampton's "born cowboys" who howled and waved sheets and shot in the air, stampeding twenty-five hundred animals from their corral on the James River back to the hungry Confederate side. For a brief time, Sawney and his comrades ate well.

Yet cold weather brought renewed hardship. He saw comrades put their frozen feet down in the blood of a cow, pull the hide up around their ankles, and cut off strips of hide to tie it there. The only equipment the regiment obtained was enemy loot. They had little to put in their mouths but tobacco and onions. The chewing habit fastened itself on Sawney's nature. He lived on a nameless emotion that displaced despair. His promotion to first sergeant could mean but little.

Sad news came from home in early 1865. William Bingham was moving the school to Mebane Station. Without a railroad, he could get no supplies at Oaks. Shortages and inflation had already made family boarding at reasonable rates impossible. William's failing father was violently opposing the move. Old Bingham ordered the family slaves to ignore his son's requests. Frail William Bingham went on trying to teach and carry out his plans. His younger brother Robert was away in the war.

Sawney was witness to mutinies as well as to desertions, and even to a conspiracy to kill his own colonel. He saw fifty men hung up by their thumbs until they fainted. Comrades died by his side and fell at his feet. Rebel lines were crumbling. His final battle of the war was the stand at Namozine Church. Field promotions quickly made him captain now. He commanded the Second Cavalry's right wing. Twice in these confused hours he almost perished in the rear guard action. An overwhelming Federal force caught him at a bridge. A Yankee raised his sword to crown him with death. The quick little Confederate whipped a pistol from his belt and shot his enemy. It was the only time Sawney was certain he killed a man. He lost his beloved mare Electricity when a Yankee shot her out from under him.

On April 3 at Amelia Courthouse, a few mounted soldiers in gray approached Sawney's brigade commander. They were not Confederates, they were spies. A troop of blue suddenly galloped in behind them. General Rufus Barringer surrendered and Captain Webb was captured during the night. The next morning, without an invitation, young Webb declined a Yankee breakfast, although he was facing a forty-five-mile march. The prisoners set out for Petersburg, under guard, General Barringer alone being allowed to take his horse. The narrow roads were full of advancing Federals. Sawney struggled through ditches and briars, and around stumps. He was worn, heartbroken, nearly starving, humiliated by capture and defeat. "I do not think I could have survived . . . had not Gen. Barringer, although an older man, often given me a ride, and walked among the rubbish of the roads." At City Point, seven miles from Petersburg, Sawney was interrogated. A Union captain went down the ragged gray line. "I was astounded at the number who turned then and there and had themselves recorded as deserters. . . . I answered that I was a prisoner of war. It was a serious thing. . . . They threatened me with the Dry Tortugas." To a righteous Unionist, did not Sawney's southern loyalties indict him as a diehard Rebel traitor? He was herded into the hold of a small vessel for a trip north. A white officer from Boston was in charge and Negro soldiers were the guards.

Sawney recalled, "I pledge you my word that when they crowded us on that ship there wasn't room to squat, much less sit down, and then when we put out to sea each fellow had to pay his tribute to Neptune. Yes, sir, right down the other fellow's back. . . ." There were hundreds of sick fellows. They found it unbearable below. "On the way we Confederates captured the ship, disarming our Negro guard, and throwing many of the arms overboard. Finding we didn't have enough water to reach Cuba, we put the arms in charge of the captain of the ship and promised we would police it properly. . . ." Sawney recalled being at sea about three days. "When we reached the Harbor of New York we heard of Lee's surrender. The prisoners were released as fast as they would take the oath of allegiance." Sawney's heart was not a weathercock of loyalties. When he could pledge allegiance again, it would be neither false nor meaningless.

On April 11, 1865, the prisoners debarked at windswept Hart's Island—Sawney recalled it had not then one sprig of green. It lay in the westernmost waters of Long Island Sound. He was one of 592 new prisoners. About 800, most of them physical wrecks, had arrived from New Bern the day before. More than 2,000 worn-out captives had come from City Point three days before that.

It was Plague Island—pneumonia, dysentery, scurvy, smallpox, measles, erysipelas, and other diseases. Almost 2,000 needed medical treatment, and 217 of these patients died. Meager hospital-tent facilities were overwhelmed. A medical inspector reported the pattern: men poorly clad and exhausted, weather cold and damp, no bedding, crowded and unventilated barracks. Sawney remembered "the guard would use his bayonet & make us 'spoon up' until he got sometimes 6 or 8 in one bunk. . . ." At first, according to the inspector, breathing space per man was less than the volume of a five-foot cube. One side of the long barracks was the prison wall—without either doors or windows. Yet Sawney could write his family that his own health remained "unimpaired." Prisoners were allowed to bathe and fish in the bracing salt water that lapped a sandy beach on the eastern shore of the island shaped like a pair of spectacles. Sawney did not miss practicing the bath habit he was certain had enabled his frail body to survive.

His fellow prisoners were of all classes on earth—gamblers, drunkards, even bounty jumpers who had sold themselves for $1,000 several times to take the place of draft evaders. Sawney claimed these were Yankees in disguise who after deserting had managed to trade for enough gray clothes to fool the inspector. A card sharp became Sawney's permanent bunkmate, "& while my bedfellow was organizing a gambling den, I was organizing a YMCA & our prayers & profanity went up to heaven together. . . ." Sawney, however, did not preach to him, and the sharp stopped cussing in front of his religious companion.

There was no mess hall, and the rations were handed out—more accurately, tossed out—as Sawney remembered: "There was no con-

trol of the men there and no defense of property rights, even in so
much as a cracker. . . . As soon as anybody bought anything at the
bursar's, the garroters jumped on him and took it away. . . . These
'garroters,' as we called them, organized for robbery and plunder."
They tried to throttle a muscular 250-pounder named Steele. As he
let loose with his fists, a garroter dropped at every punch. "When
he had knocked down about seven or eight they were retiring and
Steele put that shovel of a hand of his on a victim's head and mashed
him down between his knees, then with a broad smile he turned
him over and spanked him good. Then the crowd, 2,000 of us,
backed him. . . .

"We had to organize a government, pass laws, and assign penal-
ties," Sawney remembered, "and for months that was the best government I ever lived under." Sawney was appointed centurion and
prosecuting attorney "although I had never read a law book in my
life."

Crowding diminished and conditions improved as more of the
prisoners took the oath. Sawney himself delayed swearing allegiance
until after the last Confederate commander surrendered in early
June. Then he was shipped several hours south to a temporary
prison at the battery on the lower tip of Manhattan Island. Here
the soldier found a comic way to cap four years of tragedy and pain.

Near the giant stone pillbox known then as Castle Garden, a parapet stretched some distance out into the water. On pretext of bathing one morning, he dived around the parapet. Before the guard
could run to the other side, Sawney had disappeared up Broadway
into its pedestrian and horse-drawn traffic. Seventy cents in silver
were left in his pocket. His Aunt Maggie, who was living in Ohio,
had thoughtfully sent him twenty Yankee dollars. He made straight
for the famous attraction that had excited his boyhood imagination:
Barnum's Museum. Admission to Barnum's cost a quarter.

There were "seven grand salons" and some "850,000 curiosities,"
but the live-animal exhibits impressed him most. He never forgot
a repulsive yellow beast called an "ichneumon" that kept annoying
and pestering a duck and a cat in an otherwise "happy family"
group. At the boa constrictor's glassed-in cage, "my eyes suddenly
came upon him with his head turned back, and his tongue sticking
out, and I smashed the glass cage behind me." A crowd gathered
around this disheveled youth in the wet greasy uniform he had
worn for months. A Federal soldier took hold of Sawney's button.

" 'This is a Confederate button.' Said I, 'yes.' He says, 'Your clothes are wet.' Said I, 'Yes.' Said he, 'If they were dry, I believe it would be Confederate gray. . . .' Said I, 'I am a Confederate soldier; I escaped from prison this morning, and I know, or do not doubt, that you would get a large reward if you would arrest me and take me back.' This was met with a large guffaw of derisive laughter. . . ."

Sawney tried a theater next, buying a seat in the gallery. As he stepped through a door at the top of the corridor, he stumbled and fell on the steep steps, again attracting much attention. Another Federal officer recognized him for a Rebel, and cries of "Put him out!" came from all parts of the building. Sawney's frail little-boy look now served him well. "A number of women gathered around me and gave me the program and said they should not put me out. . . ." Asked again whether he really was a Confederate soldier, he again admitted having escaped, and again provoked derisive laughter.

He had a dime left. "By night I was hungry," he recalled. "I took a seat in a Broadway restaurant, with marble top tables, and examined a very large menu." Finding nothing for a dime, he asked a pretty waitress for ten cents' worth of bread. She said it was a strange order. " 'Well,' said I, 'I will have to go. . . .' " Again he was identified, admitted being a Rebel, and was the butt of incredulous amusement. But the girl whispered that she herself was a Georgia refugee—he could not fool her—that he should keep his seat—"and she brought me a supper the likes of which I had never seen. . . . By midnight I was tired, without any money. . . ."

He decided to escape back. There were no lights at the large wagon gate of the prison except one candle, with one green soldier on guard. "As he turned his back, in walking his beat," Sawney said, "I stepped across the line and asked him please to let me go out on Broadway. He cursed me with great violence into the prison. . . ."

In July, the last of the Rebels were returning South.

V. Reconstruction:
To Wear the Face
God Gave Me

Learn one thing at a time.
That's all Solomon could do.
—SAWNEY WEBB

His homecoming is almost lost in legend. He made his way south by rail. He rode for a stretch in an open flatcar. His tattered cap flew off in the wind. He reached his mother and sisters in mid-summer, with his only clothes on his back. He went to bed while they took the greasy uniform he had worn for months and boiled it thoroughly.

"I didn't have money enough to buy me a hat . . . to buy me a coat," he remembered. "My sisters took straw out of the strawsack and platted me a hat, and it was done well, too. I went to a lady that sewed and I asked her to take that coat that I had worn in the army and rip it up and turn the greasy side inside and make me a new coat. I didn't want to go to see any girls in that coat. I couldn't!"

Sawney recalled that the sewing lady laughed at him: "It won't fit," she said.

"Oh, yes!" Sawney said. "I have studied geometry and symmetry.

You can put this piece over there and that one over here . . . and it's bound to fit."

She laughed at him again and refused the job. Sawney went on a neighbor's horse to another sewing lady, about eight miles away. "You rip the coat up and I will come back when you've finished it and I will show you how to put it back together." On his return, Sawney found she had already re-sewed it into a decent-looking coat. "Of course it fit," he said. "I had studied my geometry before the war."

Being home was good beyond all expression. Every Webb had survived. Yet it was a hungry year. Home was hardly the same. The Binghams, whose academy had brought the Webbs to Oaks twenty years before, were gone. W. J. Bingham, Sawney's old teacher, was so broken by tragedy that friends talked sadly of his having gone insane. In early 1866, Old Bingham died.

That same winter, Sawney started a school at home. "I had *individuality*. . . . I did not think there was any other place in the universe to live." He advertised. He declined repeated invitations from John E. Dugger to become a junior partner in teaching school at Warrenton, even when Dugger, future superintendent of Raleigh schools and future university trustee, made a fifty-fifty trial proposition. "For a month I had one pupil," Sawney said. "The first year I did not get enough pupils to pay my board." He considered going west, to Henderson, Kentucky, even to California. He wrote inquiries. An uncle replied that if Sawney had written sooner he might have organized a school in Memphis for the 1866 fall session, paying $200 to $250 a month. In mid-September, he was offered a half-time teaching job at $60 per month plus board. His wartime employer, James H. Horner, wanted him back at Oxford. Sawney accepted.

However, he did not arrive October 1, as Captain Horner asked. That very day, Sawney was busy on the Oaks farm having the corn crib moved. Besides teaching, he worked the land along with ex-slaves Stephen and Doc. Sawney would return to Ma, Suny, and Addie during vacations. They needed a man's protection as well as help. He arrived at Horner's October 6, bringing Sam and two Memphis cousins as students.

Oxford, North Carolina, was a neat little town, the Granville County seat, with freshly painted houses. Everything about nearby Horner Hill was large scale. The two-story house slept and boarded as many as twenty-one students besides the Horner family. Some of the boulders about the yard stood as high as the house itself.

James Hunter Horner was almost six-and-a-half-feet tall. His handsome wife Sophronia Moore Horner, a relative of the Webbs, was proportionately ample in stature and in heart, which kept her cheerfully going eighteen hours a day. Captain Horner had the reputation of working twelve hours a day. Though desks and backed chairs were proudly advertised school equipment, any chair he sat in seemed too small. Horner had a full head of coarse hair, shaggy eyebrows, a magnificent Roman nose, and large eyes. He walked with the style of a thoroughbred. Sawney's first and only employer highly impressed him at the beginning. He praised Horner's "originality" and engaged him in the bloodless war of chess. People believed Old Bingham had rightly pronounced alumnus James Horner a genius. The infectious spirit of play he brought to learning sometimes led to spontaneous applause when a student favorite succeeded in answering a hard question in the fast-moving game of trapping, or "tripping," as it was known at Horner's.

His greatest defect as a teacher was his inability to tolerate dullards. He taunted them with the younger boys of nimble brain. When a big youth missed and an infant genius answered right, Horner baited the loser like this: "Now, sir. Aren't you ashamed, sir; this little fellow, sir, no higher than your knees, sir! could swallow you whole, sir! without greasing your head, sir! or, even pinning back your ears, sir!" Little intellectual cannibals stuffed themselves full at Horner's. Occasionally, however, a muscular youth of spirit took the abuse no longer. Horner and the big boy flew into combat, wrestling about the platform or floor. Quickly the schoolmaster would come to his senses, and fall into a chair, almost fainting with apparent shame. No one accused him of malice or meanness. Bright boys took liberties with impunity.

Sawney's youngest brother Sam, soon after his arrival, asked permission to go sightseeing downtown. Horner, adhering to a rule forbidding it, suggested that Sam go see a creek in the opposite direction. At supper Horner asked boarder Sam if he had seen the creek. "Yes, sir," Sam replied, "and if Oxford isn't any better looking than the creek, I advise you to grease it and let the dogs lick it up."

Mornings before school, boys played around under trees, on boulders, and at the edge of a peach orchard. When they saw Horner and

Company coming, they yelled "Faculty! Faculty! Faculty!" Then they disappeared over the stile and into the T-shaped schoolhouse.

Early in the 1867 winter term, Sawney's Memphis cousin Graham was a top scholar in the sophomore class. Sawney had taught him for only eight months, while Graham's fellow students had been studying at Horner's for a year and a half. His performance was a factor in raising his older cousin's salary.

Now "Captain Webb" was full-time, teaching seven hours a day, working and studying extremely hard when recurrent chills and fever did not down him. Students responded to the scrawny little man's thoroughness and drive. His pay was perhaps the best in the state: more than $150 a month—at the rate of $2,000 a year. The school was flourishing, with almost a hundred students. Horner excited his new assistant with promises. He talked of going to Memphis and starting a school there. Who but Sawney would be his successor at Oxford? Later he gave Brother John an advance invitation to teach, and said the Brothers Webb could have the school in a few years, when he planned to retire.

Sawney was enthusiastic about helping his younger brothers. Brother Dick wrote Sam to be grateful to Sawney "for his arduous efforts to have you educated." Sawney told John to charge to him whatever he needed at Chapel Hill. He also wrote John that he would waive his priority as an older heir to the family estate, in the interest of John's pursuit of learning. The Person County acreage had been sold, and money became available periodically as Brother James was able to collect it.

Praises of Sawney's teaching were "unanimous," according to Sawney's old teacher at Chapel Hill, Professor "Fatty" Phillips. The faculty of the state university awarded him his A.B. in the spring of 1867, and his A.M. the following year.

The young assistant was learning to make a game of discipline. One winter's night Horner awoke Sawney in his upstairs room and told him there was a disturbance among the boarders. "I got up and dressed very leisurely," Sawney recalled. "When I went around to the rooms, every fellow was in bed and snoring. I just went to each room with a basket and took every pair of shoes that had snow on them. They had been out snowballing. . . . The next morning you ought to have seen the boys come down to breakfast"—without their shoes.

He also developed an eye for the defeated boy. A day student

stammered, and rode to school on a dilapidated gray horse. Other
boys laughed at him. He fell apart in the rapid game of trapping.
Sawney, according to a family story, called the dejected boy aside
and said, "Wilbur, I'm going to give you just one task—I want you
to learn the first rule of Bingham's *Latin Grammar,* 'The subject of
a finite verb is in the nominative case.' It will keep you off foot of
the class." With great pains, the boy learned the rule, and enjoyed
a momentary success. "Wilbur," Sawney said, in a follow-up, "I
want you to learn a second rule." The young stammerer went on
learning "one thing at a time." In fact, he made a distinguished
career for himself in the learned world.

Sawney did find Horner's an intellectually stimulating place. On
Friday afternoons, assemblies heard distinguished speakers, members of the local bar, and youthful orators. Townspeople, as well as
the students, attended these programs. Although Sawney could not
agree with some of his employer's methods, he endorsed for life one
of Horner's express principles of education: "The popular and mercenary system of dispensing with all studies which cannot be turned
to a practical and lucrative account is, in our opinion, one of the
principal causes of that narrow-mindedness, infidelity, and fanati-
cism, which have brought upon our country so many calamities."

Sawney did some hard thinking and one Friday afternoon he decided it was time he made his debut as a public speaker. He would
face the weekly assembly of townspeople and the students. "I saw
a vision of the fields that had been wet with the blood from my
body," he recalled. In the school auditorium, raw-boned, clean-
shaven, scrawny-looking Captain Webb, with shy eyes and a hunch
in his right shoulder, spoke up for lasting peace on earth. He called
for an international court that would adjudicate differences between nations, and prevent horrible wars like the one he had managed to survive.

He knew his spirit had succumbed to audience skepticism: "The
people greeted me with guffaws and laughter." Both lawyers and
judges ridiculed his proposal. One old Justice explained to the hurt
young man: "When I decide a question, I have a sheriff and the
other officers of the county to enforce my decree. Now . . . in an
international court where is your army to stand behind the decisions of the court? . . . They can't enforce their decisions." It would
be years before the sensitive young man could be persuaded to give
a speech in public again.

Other ventures Sawney made at Oxford also had dispiriting results. En route he had bought for $15 a suit of "shoddy" that quickly
fell apart. In the winter of 1867 he was buying new clothes, and suit
material that cost $12 a yard. Sam thought he must be "fixing to
get married." After months of moving about in society, he wrote in
misery to his younger sister Addie: "You know that I always go
blundering through life, making myself ridiculous and doing awkward things, and still am not happily oblivious of them, but pain-
fully conscious and peculiarly sensitive." He asked a young lady to
attend commencement at Chapel Hill with him. She accepted, then
reneged. He wrote Addie he would not attend the commencement
at all. "Sawney dear, *brother of my heart*," Addie wrote, "If you
give weight to *girls' remarks*, dear Sawney, you will be in many a
quandary before you die. Most of them speak from impulse of the
moment. . . . Neither allow y'r vanity to be flattered nor y'r spirits
depressed, & under all, & everything, reserve the glorious privilege
of being *independent*. I *would* attend commencement even if she
did, or did *not*. Don't flatter her vanity. . . ."

His older sister Susan kept nagging him to give up his war habit
of chewing tobacco. She tried the feminine tactic that he loved the
tobacco more than he did her. She worried about Sam. He was
homesick, weeping, and complaining over how long and hard he
had to work. The heavy work students did at Horner's was impressive to Sawney. He had never seen anything quite like it. Susan considered it want of "discretion." A growing boy that missed sleep
could ruin his health. She cited to her brother Old Bingham's dictum: "Short lessons thoroughly learned."

The lonely young teacher found strength and solace in his religious faith. He regularly attended the preaching of the circuit rider
who had baptized him. John Tillett, later known as the "Iron Duke
of the Methodist Itinerancy," was a powerful broad-nosed fellow
with burning eyes. He admitted that "the natural man in him" had
been greatly tempted by a prize-fighter's career. He prayed for "that
violence of spirit which takes the Kingdom of Heaven by force."
Before the war Tillett had fearlessly attacked slavery, especially the
slave trader who heartlessly separated husband and wife, parent and
child, in pursuit of maximum profit. He himself was forced to farm
in order to support both his family and his religious calling. He was
also a "Puritan of the Puritans" in his attitude toward popular
amusements, and his young parishioner Sawney Webb persisted

in attending school dances as a faculty member, even though he did not personally join in the easy-going Episcopalianism of his employers.

One morning, with Captain Webb in Amen Corner, Tillett preached a Bill of Attainder sermon against the young teacher. His text was Mark 14, which describes the disciple Peter warming himself by the fires of Christ's enemies. At the climax, the "Iron Duke" roasted young Sawney by denouncing any professing Christian "who would attend wine parties and champagne suppers, but would not himself drink, who would watch gamblers at their games but would not himself gamble, who would go to dances and card parties, but would not himself dance or play cards." Sawney never forgot the personal roasting, though he continued to do what he deemed his duty. He also grew more and more uncomfortable at Oxford.

Certain that an old sweetheart at Oaks had gone back on him, he started calling on a local "beauty." She captivated him. "I did not see the art . . . I liked to have blundered fatally." Then a grandmotherly friend of the Widow Webb sent for him, and successfully warned him against the girl—and the girl's family.

By the winter of 1868, the economic effects of Reconstruction had sent school enrollment tumbling fifty per cent. From one session to another, Brother Sam's class dropped from thirty to six in number.

Captain Webb and his fellow teaching assistant Captain Alexander Redd, both of them similarly "dried up and poor looking" in young Sam's brutal eyes, took long walks together evenings. They were unsuccessfully trying to acquire a school together at Wilmington. Redd's being a Baptist made it impossible in a society of competing sects, and he subsequently became a professor at Chapel Hill.

Sawney no longer had confidence in Horner, or in Horner's promises. By the last of April, 1868, he was offering Sawney $500 for the July–December session. As April became May, Horner reneged: "Today he has made me a different proposition and perhaps will make a half dozen more before the end of the session," Sawney wrote to John. However, he insisted that John spare no expense to obtain good books.

In a time of chaos, no one could live abundantly, or prosper. "Reconstruction in North Carolina," declared Sawney, "was worse than war. . . . Bandits made no concealment in those days. . . . Neighbors

plundered neighbors. . . . I did not dare go away from home un-
armed; I did not know when I was going to be seized. When a ban-
dit sees you armed, he lets you alone, unless he gets the drop on
you. . . . There were five barns burned in my neighborhood. . . . The
horse I drove in the army was stolen out of a plow, in broad, open
daylight . . . and the only opportunity to recover the horse was to
take him at the point of a pistol. I was the only protector of my
mother and two sisters. While I would be in one part of the farm,
the fattening hogs would be stolen out of the other part."

Sawney wrote his mother in 1869 that a "scalawag" judge in
Oxford, "from the numerous cases of hogstealing," conceded that
a hog would become so rare in a few years as to be carried about
like a circus animal. "A great bunch of robbers came up to my
mother's home," Sawney recalled. "They had gone to other homes
and robbed them and burned them. I told them that the first man
that put his foot in that gate would be a dead man and they knew
it. I wouldn't have stood there for myself . . . I wouldn't have stood
there for the property . . . but I stood there for my mother."

Without property, farm people starved. Sawney could take no
broad view—from vantage points of decades, or regions, away. He
lived inside the hide of a former Confederate soldier with a war
throb in his shoulder, the bitter reality of lands and homes burned
into desolation, the awareness of the lacerated emotions of war-
bereaved women and children, the bitter memory of Yankee use
of blacks as instruments of threat and violence, the present use of
blacks for political purposes, the largest expropriation without the
slightest compensation of legally recognized property in human history, his family homestead right now under constant threat, and his
own person in danger of violence whenever he went abroad. Everybody seemed to go armed. When a bushel basket of pistols were col-
lected from Horner students, the youths themselves resented their
loss of privilege.

Perverse white resentment arising from the social guilt of slavery
tangled with the terror of racial violence come true and a feeling
that associated the black presence with all the region's troubles. The
"nigra" became a hateful abstraction where love and even admiration between individual white and black strangely survived and
privately managed to prevail. Yet white rationalizations that black
people were inherently inferior hardened into conviction. White
southerners, even those who believed in the Gospel of Love and the

Prince of Peace, were conditioned to live with the spiritual scars of violence and hate—their minds bound and limited by ethical confusions of injustice compounded with injustice, painful humiliation still stinging with vindictive pride—an obsession with unforgiven wrong that has perpetuated the creation of hell on earth and in the human heart throughout the history of recorded time.

Sawney could not imagine the human anguish on the other political and social side of Reconstruction. He was too involved as breadwinner, family protector, and provider for his younger brothers' education. He was too much a continuing part of the human tragedy. He blamed "carpetbaggers and native thieves" and the "help of the Negroes." And he knew that law enforcement had completely broken down.

However, he would not wear a white robe, or a mask. "I never propose to wear any face but the one God gave me" was a lifetime motto. He resisted pressures to join the Ku Klux Klan: "I wouldn't join them because they went in disguise. A Northern general asked me what I thought about men who would go about doing things in disguise. I told him I thought they were arrant cowards. I also said that I despised the Boston Tea Party in my very soul. . . ." As a brother of three merchants, he had reason to feel sorry for the owners of the tea. "I told [the Klan] that if they would go about their work of restoring order in the daytime and without disguise, I would work with them and stand the consequences, even if it were a penitentiary sentence, but I would not go about at night and in disguise. . . ."

Reconstruction was also fragmenting John's formal education. He had gone from Bingham's Mebaneville campus to the state university and had immediately won sophomore standing. The atmosphere, however, was no encouragement to learning. John wrote his family about the tolling of the bell and the tarring of the "Fresh" seats the evening a Yankee general brought to the campus as his bride the daughter of President (former Governor) Swain. John also reported students' preparing an effigy to hang, when word reached Chapel Hill that the radical state governor William "Weathercock" Holden planned a visit.

University attendance dropped. Radicals despised the institution as a white refuge for unreconstructed Southerners. Ex-Confederate diehards despised Swain as a Yankee's father-in-law. Students like John questioned "Gov" Swain's intellectual qualifications. Academic standards dropped. John wrote Brother Sam in the spring of 1868: "The Gov has the Seniors on Lossing's 'Pictorial Common School History of U. S.' and Charles Phillips has been lecturing on Arithmetic. Isn't it a farce!"

John wanted dearly to attend the University of Virginia, but Sawney and his merchant brothers could not afford the extra expense. Sam needed financing too. Sawney wanted him to go on to Washington College in Virginia, where General Lee was the president. On suspension of instruction at Chapel Hill in the summer, John was easily first in the junior class. Now he was forced to seek a teaching post. Susan complained that John looked like a "hot house plant" for want of exercise. That fall he was ill. By early 1869, however, he was on Colonel Bingham's faculty at Mebaneville. "He does his work faithfully and efficiently," William Bingham wrote Sawney at the end of March, "& accomplishes all I expect of him, but his position is an unpleasant one, and he has become depressed & discouraged beyond measure, so as to talk seriously of quitting his post. He imagines that he does not command the respect of the boys and feels with a keenness which none but a very sensitive nature knows, the little differences in demeanor which boys make between myself & him."

Sawney wrote to John in a hurry: "Don't become discouraged in spirit. If you find yourself brooding over difficulties, bury y'r thoughts in some mathematical problem or some book or pay a visit—anything to get away from y'r thoughts. We are just alike, haven't enough self-confidence and hence under[r]ate ourselves. We must struggle against it with all our might. With prayer to God, we may be able to overcome every obstacle that is in our path."

They had already decided to join forces and Sawney had acknowledged John to be the intellectual "star": "In consequence of my failure to finish my course . . . I will have to do drudgery all my days and stick to the grammar & dictionary. You will have to do the polishing for the firm of Webb & Company."

At Horner's in the fall of 1869, Captain Webb and a fellow teacher expatiated on an educational Utopia. Their lively imaginations conjured up the vision of a Great University. It would elevate the mental status of the world. The German universities of the time were "mere nothings" in comparison. Meanwhile they coped with intolerable realities.

By 1870, Sawney was determined to move west. He armed himself with recommendations from former teachers and established what contacts he could. It almost broke his heart to be leaving home so far behind, but he was sick of almost everything else in his native state. He hungered for independence and a change. By late spring he was aboard a railroad train facing unknowns across the Alleghenies.

VI. Rather than Imprison
Innocent Children

My heart sinks
when I reflect upon
how immortal minds have been treated
in this vicinity.
—SAWNEY WEBB

The remarkable Iron Horse was unrolling such magnificent pictures the young teacher could not sleep. The blossoming earth swept by his window—hundreds and hundreds of miles of it. Sawney counted off amazing distances. The rails swung into a grand circle of the compass for the plunge across the Alleghenies, with a northeasterly run into Virginia, a western turn to Lynchburg, then a spectacular winding and puffing south among the mountains, tracking "ravines & creeks and branches & cracks and crevices" and plunging four times through the roaring dark of tunnels before reaching the Tennessee line at Bristol.

The journey to Knoxville produced the garden-green of his native Carolina mountains, then "an occasional glimpse of the Cumberland[s] on my right"—until Chattanooga, where both mountain masses came together—"then such windings does the Iron Horse make to find his way . . . with the broad Tenn[essee] River on one side and mountains hanging over the track on the other." A final

night-rollicking across the foothills, "the wealthiest country," took
Sawney to Decatur in north-central Alabama near the Tennessee
line. He quit counting mileages. So far the strange reconnaissance
had not cost him thirty dollars. "I think the beautiful scenery fully
pays me for my trip," he cheerfully wrote his mother. His rational
mind gave him little hope that the journey could take him very far
professionally. The land of men was not so beautiful.

The South was a backward and blighted country, much of its soil
impoverished by one-crop farmers, most of its man-made wealth
burned or wrecked by northern practitioners of total war or by
southern vandals, the archaic body-politic lacerated by abortive social revolutionaries or by fast-buck artists, both southern and northern, and now being roughly patched together into a society of caste
and race by the only men strong and capable enough to impose and
sustain any kind of order upon a hostile and resentful people. The
follies of prolonged violence demoralized tens of thousands of the
young. Children "just out of their trundle beds," copying a habit
of many grown-ups, were seen and reported drunk and staggering
down unpaved village streets. Sullen youths spoke a disorderly language, and ran out of control all over the countryside, brawling,
fighting, and resisting authority.

What education there had been was generally a shambles. State
school inspectors found dilapidated shacks with doors missing, windows shattered, holes in roofs and walls, children sometimes seated
on the floor and using backless benches as the only writing sur-
faces available. Many better-housed schools were educational shams.
There were dozens of "colleges," but they took students of all ages
from ten-year-olds up. The "president" of one was also its entire
faculty. Public schools hardly existed. So far as Sawney could learn,
not one school west of the Alleghenies, from the lakes to the gulf,
private or public, confined its curriculum to college preparation.

He wrote his mother he expected to be home in two weeks. He
traveled a little in Kentucky, more in Alabama and Mississippi, and
most in middle Tennessee: "I tried Columbia, Murfreesboro, Pu-
laski, and Gallatin. . . ." Everywhere he went, school boards saw a
frail-looking 130-pounder with a strange way of holding a dan-
gling right arm, who unsuccessfully tried to hide a little-boy face
behind a hastily grown mustache. He was a shy one to be wearing a
schoolmaster's black coat-tails, high starched collar, and bow tie.
He hardly looked the twenty-seven years he was. His hair was red-

dish, but the brawn was lacking: big, unruly schoolboys had to be mastered by physical force.

What could the extravagant praise of Webb's testimonials mean? Who, pray, was this Professor Phillips, "late" of the University of North Carolina? Even the name Bingham at this date could mean little to most of the local men Sawney met in his travels. Everywhere, he found negative, disbelieving faces.

Then he heard about a "University of Culleoka" in Maury County, only ten or twelve miles south of Columbia. The village nestled along the Nashville-Decatur railroad line, among the limestone hills, just north of the trestle over meandering Fountain Creek. *Culleoka* was Indian for "sweet water." Sawney Webb stepped off the train at the wooden box of a depot called Pleasant Grove, about half a mile north of the village, and soon faced a dozen members of the Culleoka "Institute's" Board of Trustees. They examined his testimonials. They looked at his own statement. They looked at him. Sawney heard the same discouraging word he had heard elsewhere, from a giant of a farmer with a broad face and hands as big as hams: "You are too young to take charge of our boys and girls, so I shall vote against you." Sawney remembered replying, "I have two purposes in life, one is to get married and the other is to get a school. To get a school, it is to my interest to look old in experience, and to get a girl, it is to my interest to look young in appearance, so Mr. Taylor, I have put on my young looks hoping that you would give me a school so that I could get married."

Claiborne Taylor greatly admired the ladies. Sawney never forgot the scene, or Taylor's kindly eyes as the farmer said, "If that's the case, I am going to vote for you." First, he tested the young man on a problem in cubes—involving the capacities of corn cribs of different sizes. Sawney quickly produced a quantity. "Well," Taylor said, "you are the first teacher that I ever examined that gave me a correct answer. . . . I can work anything in figures." Sawney challenged his examiner with a problem that required calculus to solve: If a rabbit jumps from his bed exactly one hundred yards north of a dog and runs directly east and the dog chases him with his nose toward the rabbit all the time and catches him when the rabbit has run a hundred yards, how far has the dog run? The young teacher was amazed to watch this middle-aged farmer, with two weeks of formal schooling in his life, improvise a method like calculus to come very near the solution. Claiborne Taylor and his pretty wife became Sawney's best friends as long as they lived.

On June 20 the Reverend Mr. Billy Wilkes of Culleoka wrote the young job-hunter that the secretary of the board would inform him officially of his election as principal. If the trustees had dreamed of the impact this shy-looking young man would make on the community, some of them never would have voted for him. Wilkes was sure that Webb could raise tuition "without serious objection" if his performance gave "anything like the satisfaction that your testimonials would justify in expecting." He also vaguely promised a better school-building in the future. But in answer to Sawney's question, he doubted the school could pay enough for a "joint principal." Even maximum tuition was only a quarter a day per student—$25 for a twenty-week session, and parents with more than one child received a generous discount. It was a mad idea, but Sawney persisted in keeping his brother John in mind. On Independence Day in 1870, W. R. (Sawney) Webb wrote his acceptance letter to the Culleoka board.

The new principal was forced to obtain a young lady assistant of intellectual competence. He chose one on whom he had made calls at Chapel Hill, Miss Robina Mickle, the sister of Joe Mickle, Sawney's academic rival at every school he had attended. Romantic gossip buzzed back home. He also published a one-page school circular, asked the trustees to send it around, spent a total of $43.50 on advertising announcements in county weeklies and in the Methodist *Christian Advocate.* Alone, he faced the crucial year of his life. He opened Culleoka Institute the first week of August, 1870.

He entered his "schoolhouse." It was a damp, gloomy basement. Blue-green moss grew on the dirt walls. It contained rude benches and a stove. Sawney recalled that "after a rain, we swept it with a spade." Prospective students would come, take one look at the hole in the ground, and leave. So much for the equipment.

Sawney found a conglomeration of pupils that ranged from fully developed young men and women to shrill-voiced youngsters just beginning their ABC's. In the first-day confusion he managed to assign lessons in all categories: "I taught Virgil, Ovid, Caesar, Beginner math, everything." In the period just before mid-day, he called on the highest class to see what progress they had made in a physics book they had chosen for themselves. "We are not going to recite before dinner, we are going to recite after dinner," he was told. So the pupils here were accustomed to governing the teacher instead of the teacher's governing the pupils? "I met the issue," Sawney remembered, "and it required the threat of physical force to make them come to the recitation bench." They recited *before* their mid-day meal.

The next day he called first for the class in Caesar. Four charming girls about fourteen came forward with perfect confidence. Sawney asked one to read. She pronounced the Latin words without regard to vowel quantities. "Translate," the teacher said. The four girls looked embarrassed. "Give me the English to the Latin," he explained.

"That is not the way," the girls replied.

"What *is* the way?"

"We read the Latin and the teacher reads the key," one of the girls explained.

They had never studied the grammar! This was a fraud and a sham! All of them belonged in Beginner's Latin. Let them be put back forthwith!

Before these reactions could erupt into words he thought through the consequences: he would lose the school for certain. "I put all of the Latin pupils at the beginning of Bingham's *Latin Grammar*, saying that was my habit of teaching, and continued to go through the forms of reading Caesar and Virgil, spending very little time on it. . . ." He found that the students' knowledge of mathematics was better, although it was far from accurate or thorough.

However, the weekly *Columbia Herald* reported "Prof. Webb is giving perfect satisfaction." He encouraged himself. "I have good material, better than I expected. I have 34 pupils and several engagements, enough to make as large a school as I want . . . I will have about ten boarders, have some now." The headstrong young man was harboring wild designs. He was aiming to turn this absurd classroom phenomenon into a college preparatory school in a section where hardly a genuine college existed. The Utopian dream of that ideal university remained in a corner of his young mind. A college preparatory school? A leading trustee went into peals of scornful laughter that rankled Sawney ever after. "We expect to raise here only cornfield hands," was Major Jones's response to the principal's youthful presumption.

In a short time Sawney was tangling with the entire board and with a number of villagers besides. All students not on recitation came in and out of the basement schoolroom when they pleased.

They studied out of doors if they liked. Inside, they moved their seats whenever they felt inclined, and talked to each other without penalty, provided they did all these things so as not to disturb recitations, walking quietly and talking in whispers. This procedure was unheard of in A.D. 1870. Citizens were scandalized. In about two weeks incredulous trustees and patrons called a meeting to bring the young schoolmaster to task. He well remembered the angry mouths, the vehement complaints:

"The children are just running wild up yonder."

"They don't sit in the school room."

"They are out under the trees in the shade."

Sawney spent a day discussing methods with parents. The conclusions of both board and patrons were unanimous. Webb must keep the children at their desks. Webb must remain at playtime to eat a cold lunch from a sack so as to give constant supervision. Webb must eliminate so-called study out of doors. Webb resigned. And he told them all: "Before I would imprison innocent children, I would quit the profession of teaching. I would rather make my living plowing on a steep rocky hillside with a blind mule." The patrons quickly held another meeting. Old Billy Wilkes reported to the flushed young teacher, and tried to pacify him. They would give his methods "a little further trial" if he would remain. Unsupervised outdoor study continued.

Yet this schoolmaster was not so sentimental as to think all children were always innocent: "Those who misbehaved and who failed were kept seated at desks." They were about "ten per cent" of the student body. Some youngsters "poked along" in every way. As punishment for their slowdown in changing classes, the "Professor" kept in all the boys one afternoon.

"They got restless," Sawney remembered. "Finally a big fellow got up and shouted, 'Come on boys, let's all go.' The other boys kept their seats. He looked around and then sneaked back to his seat. He was a big fellow that weighed more than forty pounds more than I did then. I went and took him by the collar and sent the other boys home. When we were alone I said, 'William G., you are an arrant coward.' "

By early fall, it was really Webb's school. At the same time, Sawney's idol, Robert E. Lee, lay dying. Sawney was sending Brother Sam at a sacrifice to a physically rundown little college named for George Washington at Lexington, Virginia, because Robert E. Lee was its president. Lee had taken the post for $1,500 a year after turning down fantastic offers of financial gain. Lee had lived as a "schoolteacher." In mid-October, the man Sawney had followed in victory and defeat died a "schoolteacher."

By then, Sawney knew he, too, could live as one: "You would be astonished to hear it said that Culleoka boasts of having the best teacher *in the state*," he wrote his mother, "and the leading businessmen say next year will fill with good citizens all the vacant houses and some new ones, people who are anxious to educate their children." The *Columbia Herald* took up the story; "Houses are in demand in Culleoka."

Back in the schoolroom, the sham of teacher-reads-the-Latin-key was virtually at an end. One day, the most advanced pupil came to the schoolmaster, and said, "I get nothing out of Virgil, what do you think about my dropping it and devoting more time to something more profitable?"

"I think it would be wise," the schoolmaster replied.

"Before the year was out," Sawney recalled, "I had just one Latin class and they had made splendid progress and were prepared by the beginning of the second term to read the Latin reader and the second year to begin Caesar."

As he began the new term in January of 1871, he had forty or more new scholars to "break in." He wrote home in general terms about the "great trouble" they gave him. "Boys used to fight me. I used to have personal fights. . . . When I first began at Culleoka I had quite a number."

Villagers wondered how this partially disabled man of so slight a build could cope with the big ones. His reflexes were unusually quick. His resourcefulness was unusually effective. He often carried a bundle of switches to the thicket where he administered "manual punishment." If a raw-boned youth twice his size attacked him, he seized the bundle by the thin end with both hands, and swung it against the hair-covered crown of his assailant's head. It stunned without harming and without marking the youth, and he told his youngest son the device had literally saved his life in these early days.

He started a public library with close to a hundred volumes in less than a year. He bought "fifty dollars worth of books without any help from anybody" for his students, who "had never read Robinson Crusoe nor the Swiss Family Robinson—never heard of such tales. . . ." He taught a Sunday school class. A regular reading club sprang up with trustee Billy Wilkes as president. A reading club at the school became a forerunner of the Webb debating societies. Young men in the village formed an active debating club.

The schoolmaster factotum stayed up to one or two o'clock in the morning. His friendly landlord "Doc" Cochran wrote Sister Susan that his *"very bad habit"* would eventually sap his constitution. Yet Sawney's health in April of 1871 was "stronger now in the spring when I usually break down than at any period of the year before." He was very happy that "my school all love me and appreciate my labors and are obedient." Enrollment had doubled to sixty-eight. "I would never have any trouble," he said, "but for the interference of parents and now they let me alone as they see I do my own way." One big problem was a persistent American attitude toward learning. "The ideals of education around me," Sawney said, "were to commercialize it. If it could not be commercialized, it was worthless." His adoption of Chapel Hill's honor system would have to wait.

Sawney was thankful to Miss "Robie" Mickle for her "incalculable service." He was sorry that she would not likely return. She was "a lady of infinite humor" and "wonderfully entertaining." He was careful not to let even his family think he might be in love with her. In the Victorian era, life for a bachelor teacher was socially precarious. It was fortunate for Sawney that his confidant, Sister Addie, had recently moved to nearby Nashville. She was now a wife and mother, and knew her dear brother needed to be safely married himself. "It was a lonely life in Culleoka," Sawney said. "Few people anywhere think as the teachers think."

Fresh fruits in season were little pleasures. "Segars" and chewing tobacco solaced his racing nerves. He found male companionship in the new "Farmers Club" and became a charter member of its executive committee. He worked at mathematical puzzles on rainy days.

In May, school examinations were held upstairs in the church auditorium. They were both oral and public. Red-faced boys in starched collars and dark suits, and quaking girls in their best cotton dresses, awkwardly mounted the platform. The *Herald* reported: "We have never heard stricter or more searching questions put to any pupils." Unfortunately, some of the children were too green and frightened to speak much above a whisper, and loud talking in the back of the church made it hard to hear. The young schoolmaster would lose no time attending to that loud talking!

Tennessee Methodism's most prominent orators made addresses. An influential organizer of the south-wide wing of the church stopped at the village. Meeting Bishop Robert Paine was one of the most fortunate events in the schoolmaker's life. Paine quickly learned where Sawney came from. Sawney recalled, "He asked me with a penetrating gaze, 'Aren't you ashamed to acknowledge that you were born in North Carolina?'" Sawney said no, explaining that he was born in Person County almost within sight of Bishop Paine's own birthplace. Paine promptly guessed who Sawney's parents were, told him his Grandmother Stanford was "the prettiest woman I ever saw," and reminisced about the swimming holes along Deep Creek and the cherry trees he once climbed around Mount Tirzah.

When Paine found out the younger man was an alumnus of Bingham's and Chapel Hill, he said, "Nobody ever had a better opportunity than yourself." On the Bishop's insistence, Sawney became his traveling companion, and drove him many miles by horse and buggy. Because Paine suffered from a cinder in his eye, Sawney read to him. The older man often stopped Sawney's reading and talked for an hour like a college lecturer. He also made it clear to Sawney that he was contemptuous of the Hallelujah, Glory-Be, Amen-shouting religious revivalism they found all about them. The Bishop was another lonely man. After a short visit home in North Carolina, Sawney learned by mid-July that Paine wanted him to teach in the bishop's home town of Aberdeen, Mississippi. A shipment of books Paine recommended reached Sawney the same month.

The Institute re-opened the first week of August, 1871, with forty-five pupils, more than the year before, and with the promise of more boarders. Bishop Paine was spreading the word, and planned to send his grandsons. Sawney always believed that the success of the Webb School was due more to Paine than to any other one man.

This young teacher was drawing on his experience at the Old Bingham school to give his own school its basic character. From Horner he derived ideas of showmanship and public relations. He had "fattened" through the year "on limestone water" and on Mrs. Cochran's board. He wrote home that "nobody can fix up things to my notion better except my own mother." Perhaps the Cochrans were presuming to treat him too much like a son, or a future son-in-law. He "never felt more vigorous," and the outlook could not have been more promising.

Before his second school year in Culleoka was out, however, the entire student body would literally disappear in less than two hours, and he would have to endure weeks of personal exile from the entire community.

VII. In Love at Last
and No Mistake

To find my room neat and in order
and somebody glad to see me
is a luxury
that I have never known much about.
—SAWNEY WEBB

The lonely schoolmaker scribbled his struggles into a quaint New England volume of blank pages. The hard cover was decorated with marbled paper and edged and backed with imitation black leather. It was invented for the student or preacher with Big Ideas. Unnumbered pages were marked alphabetically, with five for each of the twenty-six letters. As an antebellum student, Sawney had entered his references neatly, and they unmistakably spoke the young man's mind: Ambition, Contentment, Education, Friendship, God, Home, Labor (no disgrace), Liberty, Methodism, Patience, Study, and Temperance. But Sawney was turning his *Index of Subjects* into a ledger of schoolmaking experience. Little that is human remained alien to this handbook of once blank pages.

There is no record in Sawney's penciled scrawls that a farmboy ever came dragging a bony animal behind him, asking Mr. Webb whether he could "l'arn up this cow." Old Sawney's children insisted the cow incident took place at a school in the Blue Ridge

mountains. However, a hog helped settle a tuition account at Culleoka as did a desk, an axe, a stove, a table, and even a "rock." These
were Webb School's barter days. Money was scarce, collections were
difficult, and school survival chancy.

On the page with his entry "Ambition," Sawney recorded the
"Amis" family's school account. On the page where "Contentment"
referred to a poem by Horace, "Cochran, Dr. W. W." headed a list
of charges for four daughters and two sons.

Maximum tuition did not exceed $25 a term until the later years
at Culleoka, and board remained $12 a month, including lights,
washing, and other services.

On a back page were the "Incidental Expenses for the Fall Session, 1871":

Clock $7   3 doz pen staffs . . . 2 gross pens $2.50   Stove pipe $10
½ gross pen holders [$]1.00   Rent $40   15 doz copy books . . . $45.00
axe [$]1.75   80 copy books $20.00   Table [$]2.00   dictionary $5.00
3 reams paper . . . [$]12   globe $27.00   fixing stove [$]1.50   Speaker
$10   Bill for wood $20.00 . . . etc., etc.

On another page, "Proverbs in English" appeared at the top:
"I do one thing at a time" . . . "A busy man is troubled with just
one devil, an idle man with thousands. . . ." Below these words appeared school "Expenses" for the hectic spring session when Sawney
Webb was married:

Maps $18.50   Putty and putting in glass [$]2.50 labor   Desks $37.50
Cleaning privy [$]1.00   Repairing windows $3.00   Back seats $12   Ad-
vertising Herald $7.25 . . . etc., etc.

Remarkable intellectual accomplishments quickly emerged from
mundane details. "It took a long time to make people believe that
we were honest."

Sawney invited a number of men to public examinations. He
took each text, and between his fingers, gripped the pages of the
book that the class had read. " 'Now,' said I, 'gentlemen, here are
the books we are using.' I had a primary class in those days, and I
would call up one of those little tots that couldn't read and I would
take out my knife and hand it to him and tell him to open it and
stick it down in that book somewhere, and I told them I would take
the chapter, the first complete chapter of Caesar, or the first complete chapter of Cicero, that I would start on the first paragraph on
the right hand page." The public performance was impressive. The

Herald reported at Christmas time in 1871: "Questions are not put to the scholars in any regular order, and the most skeptical are convinced that there is no collusion at all between the teachers and the pupil."

There was one disharmonious note. Church trustees insisted that admission be charged for the combined girls' musical concert and boys' oratorical performance. Professor Webb balked and refused on principle. He and his music teacher, Miss Annie Ransom, believed the Christmas concert should be free to all. The trustees replied that unless they charged admission, Webb and Company could take their concert elsewhere. The school held public examinations in the church auditorium without extra expense; it could certainly help raise some money. The church wanted, and needed, a chandelier. Sawney Webb yielded—temporarily. The concert was by paid admission. The chandelier fund grew.

In the new year school enrollment was full. The board was offering to build a schoolhouse, rent it to Sawney annually for ten per cent of the costs, and make the property his after ten years. If he left earlier, the board would have the plant, and Sawney a fair rental. He wrote William Bingham for advice early in 1872. Accept "by all means" was the reply from Mebaneville—that is, if the village was desirable and if they built on a lot near which Sawney could build his own residence for "a schoolmaster should be *among* his work. . . . Pluck and brains are the two elements of success in our calling, the former including a readiness to close with work as well as with a refractory pupil,—and the latter including common sense as well as a cultivated intellect." Bingham added his hope that Sawney would continue to show those "vainglorious" Tennesseans "what a good school of the N. C. pattern is."

Adversity struck without warning one day in the spring. "When school was out in the evening, I took a walk through the woods alone. I was gone about an hour and a half. On my return, my students had gone. Those who couldn't find a train or vehicle had walked off," Sawney recalled. His Memphis relative Henry Webb, a student who also boarded at the Cochrans,' had broken out with pock-like sores. Fear of smallpox had emptied the school.

Trustee Billy Wilkes sent Sawney a written warning dated April 16: "The excitement in regard to the Small Pox will ruin your school unless Something can be done to allay it. . . . One thing is plain to me & that is whether it be *Small Pox* or not—a circulation is given to it in a way and through channels that looks at least suspicious." Nothing could be done. "The panic seized the people in the community, many of them left their homes. . . . The merchants had just gotten their spring goods and nobody in the community would come to town or pass through it," Sawney recollected. "We could get no nurse for the boy anywhere. I went to him and took charge. I had been vaccinated in my youth and had been with small pox [patients] during the Civil War. It was lonely weeks . . . for nobody would come near us to speak to us or allow us to get near enough to speak to them." The April 26 edition of the *Herald* reported, "Mr. Webb . . . is afflicted with varioloid [mild small pox] in a mild form; in consequence of which Prof. Webb's school has been dismissed until the 13th of May."

To Sawney Webb, "dismissed" was the wrong word. He took his patient fishing, "and when the fishermen saw us coming they left all the good places to us. This continued for about three weeks." At last the scare began to subside. After five weeks, Sawney remembered, every pupil had returned except one. The principal had won another battle. Maytime became a joy.

Sawney took his reconstituted student body to Nashville for the "grand" Exposition. The delighted boys and girls behaved very well until they saw a grown man who seemed no more than "twenty-two inches high," dressed in the height of fashion, with whiskers and a gold-headed cane. The children followed the midget everywhere. A pupil named Sue, who weighed over 200 pounds, led the van. Big Sue told the wee gentleman she was in love with him—had lost her heart at first sight—and begged him to come back with her to Culleoka. Sawney roared with laughter, but confessed to Sister Susan in a letter: ". . . I have made a perfect failure in the government of girls. I don't know what to do with them. They are under my management fast & brazen and I don't wish the responsibility of such characters on my hands. Such fast creatures you never saw. . . ." He learned to rely on the cooperation of their mothers.

He fell in love himself that spring. He met the girl in Nashville at Sister Addie's during the "small pox" holidays. Emma Clary of Unionville was comely and well proportioned, with clear hazel eyes and a luxuriance of braided chestnut hair. Her firm, pretty mouth— lightly creasing at the corners when she smiled—gave evidence of a sense of humor as well as determination. She was sturdy and self-reliant. When she was cut off from her family during the war, she had made her own way by copying government tax lists in her dormitory room. Her father, born during the American War for Independence, was long dead.

Addie played matchmaker. Emma Clary had been Addie's Civil War roommate at Greensboro Female College but, like Sawney, had moved from North Carolina to a Tennessee village. Addie always said Emma was the only woman she could ever imagine who would know how to handle the "dear brother of my heart." If Miss Emma found the shy, awkward schoolmaster amusing, she also found him appealing. He later told his boys that male feelings of reticence were evidence of true love for a superior woman, and a boy who found one should go calling on her until he knocked his knees off.

Soon after Sawney's visit, Addie's husband began playing Cupid by mail: "She likes you Sawney powerfully well. . . . She has spoken of you time & again and looks pleased whenever your name is mentioned. Several fellows here are after her and you had better come up & '*go get Dr. Young and have it over.*' " Dr. Young, of course, was a minister. "Don't fail to come if you can possibly get away—Miss Emma has been lonely since you left. Please burn this letter as soon as read. . . ."

In June Sawney wrote Susan: "I am in love at last and no mistake, though I think mine is a forlorn hope. . . . Now tell me what to do. Give me some of your long-headed advice. I think it was time I was acting in this matter." In less than six months Principal Webb would be thirty years old. "I am sick of living by myself."

End of term was thrown late to June 28. The *Herald* reported the school managed to close full, in spite of "small-pox, measles, and other sinister agencies." Sawney concluded that his "bitter enemy" was to blame for the near ruination of his school. It was the same Dr. Cochran who had seemed so helpful and fatherly the year before. Cochran, he said, had concealed the nature of the boy's disease. "By mail, he notified all my patrons." The reason for the sudden malice remains uncertain. The young schoolmaker was finding that his single-minded pursuit did not win him unqualified praise or universal approval.

Yet he could not have enjoyed a better press: "Prof. Webb is a Christian gentleman and highly cultivated scholar, and we felicitate the people in that vicinity on being able to induce him to locate in their midst," the Columbia weekly reported in the fall term of 1872. The school was "fast building up an enviable reputation.

. . . He already has more than a score of young men from remote sections of the state, and his prospects grow brighter."

The school became entertainment as well as news. The "beauty and chivalry" of the town and the surrounding country attended the Christmas concert. A falsetto-voiced "Miss Sue B. Anthony" gave a burlesque address on Woman's Rights, though the male pupil contoured into female shape and female clothing left certain members of the audience "cold." Now the county newspaper was reviewing the performance of Webb's school as the press today might review a play or a movie. There was, however, no paid admission this Christmas. Bull-headed "Professor" Webb had won with his principle. In January he tactfully presented the church chandelier fund with $25—enough to enable the trustees to purchase a "fine" fixture at the total cost of $125.

In January of 1873 the school opened with a record enrollment of 103, too many for one male teacher to handle. Sawney wrote John to come quickly. The younger brother, after leaving the Bingham faculty in 1870, had been teaching successfully at an academy in Rockingham, N.C. However, his work as principal there was neither satisfying nor particularly prosperous. On January 13, he wrote: "I am coming after the 'bbl. [barrel] of money.' " His older brother gave John fanfare with a paid announcement in the *Herald* on January 24: "John M. Webb has become associate Principal . . . first-honor man at the University of N. C. under the OLD FACULTY. . . . The principals hope by their joint efforts to make the school in the future more worthy of the liberal patronage with which it has been heretofore favored. Room for a few more *good* boys. . . ."

What a year 1873 was becoming! Sawney stammered out his proposal to Miss Emma the same month, and she consented to be his wife. Sawney wrote his mother: "It seems to me that I have worked hard under very great disadvantages—a lack of sympathy, and I felt that I could not stand it any longer—I have often felt so—but never met one who so completely won me as Miss Emma."

Then he catalogued her many virtues. "She has no means, yet I think I have done better than I deserved. . . . Do you think I can ever sum up courage to ask *her* mother? What do you reckon she will say when I ask for the most valuable member of her family and the youngest *too*? . . . I've no doubt that we will have great success in our school . . . nobody had so little trouble in managing a school as I now have in mine. I have of course the best *teachers*. Jno. for instance and since my return yesterday from my visit to Miss Emma I have felt that my life was a success. I have always feared until now after *all* the struggle, it would prove a failure. . . ."

Addie wrote Sister Susan: "Sawney needs a wife more than any poor boy I ever saw—He lives as scattered and careless as ever—& has been lonely . . . but if not always cheerful himself, he has a wonderful talent for making other people so."

On January 30, John Maurice Webb finally arrived in Culleoka, wearing a handsome new beaver hat. The village was abuzz. His physical proportions were closely scanned. The blue-eyed young man looked much like the first Webb, although his hair was more golden than red. He was clean shaven then, longer faced, a little taller, and more deliberate. "The boys do say he can ask more questions in hearing recitations than the older brother," the *Herald* reported almost immediately.

Within weeks, John Webb received a "rave" notice: "This young gentleman certainly understands the art of teaching; but probably we should call it a gift. . . . The pupils are not embarrassed, but seem to feel assured that the teacher is a friend, endeavoring to instruct them, instead, as is often the case, of being a tyrant to punish them. . . . The teacher did not confine himself to the book, but made plain many technical questions by familiar illustrations. The class in McGuffey's Reader was instructed by example how to read and pronounce." The more scholarly brother met a great need: "There are more large boys and advanced students in Prof. Webb's school than at any former period," added the *Herald*.

"Professor" Sawney Webb was almost beside himself with excitement. He had acquired a custom-made pair of boots for his courtship, planned to wear them to see his love, called on her, returned home, and only then noticed the new highly-polished boots exactly where he had forgotten them. Looking at his feet, he saw his plain old shoes. In late March he became ill for a day—the first time since he had come to Culleoka. He wrote Miss Emma that "they thought it was the disease of the heart. . . ." He told her it was "generally conceded *here* now that I am not to be held to a rigid accountability for what I *do* or *say*." He could not wait for the wedding two weeks away. "If I do come a week before the time won't you come back with me? I have been looking anxiously for a letter from you for more than one mail."

They were quietly married in Unionville on April 23. They

William Robert (Sawney) Webb as a Child
Courtesy of the W. R. Webb Family

"Captain" Webb during His Years
in Oxford, North Carolina
Courtesy of the W. R. Webb Family

Young Sawney in Confederate Uniform
Courtesy of the W. R. Webb Family

John Webb (left) and Sawney Webb Flank an Early Culleoka Senior Class

Courtesy of the W. R. Webb Family

The New Schoolhouse at Culleoka

Courtesy of the W. R. Webb Family

The Schoolmaker about 1875

Courtesy of Webb–Bell Buckle

*The Sawney Webb Household, Including Student Boarders,
in the Late 1870s*

Courtesy of Webb–Bell Buckle

The "Big Room" and the Bell Buckle School in the 1890s

Courtesy of Webb–Bell Buckle

Old Sawney (left) and Old Johnny, Later Known as Old Jack,
in Bell Buckle

Courtesy of Webb–Bell Buckle

Senator W. R. (Sawney) Webb in 1913, an Official Portrait

Courtesy of the W. R. Webb Family

Traditional Outdoor Study under a Bell Buckle Beech

John Webb, Scholar,
Teacher, Principal

Senator Webb, on the Speaker's Platform (left), at President Wilson's First Inaugural

Courtesy of the W. R. Webb Family

drove in a two-horse carriage to the train at Shelbyville. The bride-groom remembered the hoofbeats ringing sharply on late-frozen ground. After a couple of days' honeymoon, they arrived by train at Culleoka. Some twenty-five students were among a large crowd that cheered "the Professor and his accomplished bride." The couple reached Sawney's refurbished room at 10 P.M.

Emma was very tired, and early the next morning, when "Aunt" Mariah walked in with Sawney's woolen socks, the bride was still abed. "Emmie, can you knit?" the old servant asked. "I am gwine to spin you some yarn today, dis child [pointing at Sawney] needs some socks mighty bad." She also told the bridegroom, now that he had a wife, to treat her right. This black domestic, Aunt Mariah, gave them the only wedding present they received, a straight-handled gourd already cut for use. "She has a big soul," Sawney said.

"Everybody is delighted with Emma," he wrote his mother, "ex-cepting one fast widow, who called in a hundred dollar silk and was received in a calico dress. And *she* said she liked her *tolerably* well. . . ." Her proud husband reported after less than two weeks of mar-riage, "Emma is pretty and does pretty. Emma knows exactly how to please and she *loves to try.* . . ."

That spring he broke a public silence of several years. Since the humiliating consequences of his speech in favor of a world court, he had shied from formal addresses to mature audiences. At the Methodist District Conference in Columbia, however, he yielded to a powerfully persuasive man, Bishop Holland Nimmons McTyeire. The Bishop had, after all, just prevailed on Commodore Vanderbilt to donate a million dollars for the establishment of an institution of higher learning in Nashville. So Sawney gave a prophetic address on the importance of academies' preparing their pupils for some particular university. When the principal had finished, according to the *Columbia Herald*, McTyeire remarked in a low voice, "We have succeeded in getting a good speech out of Webb." The audi-ence did not laugh at Sawney Webb as they had at Horner's.

At commencement time in May of 1873, Culleoka was swarm-ing with visitors. Laughter greeted a vital, red-headed fatherless youth named Ned Carmack who led a "choir of boys" with combs and tissue paper in a hilarious rendition of "Rye Straw." Profes-sor Webb uneasily consented to the "profane" performance in the church sanctuary. Ned appealed to him. Ned was original. Ned was a handful. "He was the greenest boy that ever hit this school, with the exception of his hair and that was the reddest, but he wouldn't stay green, he caught on. He was always in good humor . . . he was the only boy I ever saw who had a dimple in his chin and nose both, but he worked and got the reward," the schoolmaker said.

It had been a most triumphant, joyful, and hopeful year. Sawney and Emma entrained in June for North Carolina to visit kin. That same month, however, Tennessee became alarmed, then terror stricken. A plague struck across the land "like a clap of thunder." The thirty-year-old teacher and his bride of less than three months were the only passengers aboard the Chattanooga-Nashville train on their return. The train creaked to a halt at its western terminal. Nashville was an empty silence. The couple left their lonesome car and saw only the train crew and the agent as they entered the small depot. Sawney and Emma walked ten blocks along the cobblestone streets of the Ghost City, and they saw not one human being. It was the cholera. Everyone feared one another. Through July 1, 1873, the *Union & American* reported that 647 had died of the cholera inside Nashville alone.

Sawney and Emma hurried home to Culleoka on another lonesome train. The epidemic followed them there. A fourteen-year-old girl in "Prof. Webb's school" was among the first three that died of cholera before the fourth of July. Local doctors called it the "flux." It went through families where sickness had long been unknown. The six village doctors wrote Nashville medical leaders for help and rode their horses to see the stricken, day and night. An ordained "preacher boy" who was studying at the Webb's school succumbed to the disease after sparing "no labor, no sacrifice, no exposure" in ministering to the sick. Eighteen died in a community of only a few hundred inhabitants. Sawney, Emma, and John all escaped the treacherous disease. By early August good health seemed to be returning. Cases began to yield to the usual remedies.

The younger brother studied. He wrote two eminent professors of Greek, asking them to guide him in the language for a year. One promptly and flatly refused. John heard nothing from the other, Professor James Hadley of Yale. At last a letter came from the professor's son, Arthur T. Hadley, later Yale's president, but then a student. He wrote that his father would have enjoyed guiding John Webb's reading but he had died a few days after the arrival of Webb's letter. Arthur was sending him Yale's course outlines in Greek.

On the fourth Monday of the month Sawney opened the school, with John as joint principal. However, it was a skeleton of its former self. After the cholera terror, the boarders were not returning. For a second time in little more than a year the school appeared to be on the verge of ruin.

VIII. Now This Is a Family and I Am the Father

Young men govern themselves—
boys need supervision,
restraint, and compulsion.
—SAWNEY WEBB

Emma was pregnant. Next spring Sawney would be a father. John had arrived the previous January on the promise of a growing student body. Terror and fears paralyzed the region; financial panic was sweeping the nation. Yellow fever, in the wake of cholera, was ravaging Memphis and points south.

Four "free schools" were operating that fall in Culleoka's district, three of them within three miles of Sawney's basement. A former student was teaching one of them. Sawney knew very well who had made schools important in Maury County. He would say nothing, however, to disparage the others. He never mentioned them. Yet competition just then was cruel. The day school the Webb brothers were running did not even pay expenses. "That was a blue time," Sawney recalled. Not even the Vanderbilt groundbreaking in Nashville's West End could raise his spirits. The months dragged on toward 1874.

A change began in January. Boarders were at last arriving again. Then the *Herald* reported: "Prof. Webb's school . . . opened with the largest number of pupils he has ever had on the first day of his session." By early February the student body numbered almost eighty and new scholars were continuing to arrive. The Webb School survived and prevailed once more. "Free schools" flagged. Non-paying pupils dropped out. Teachers quit in disgust. The county superintendent of schools resigned in late March. The *Herald and Mail* announced W. R. Webb's candidacy for the post in early April. No opposition to the "Professor" was anticipated. Sawney seemed to be destined for public-school administration.

A week later, the same newspaper's "Over the County" column deflated the boomlet for Webb with two quick needles: (1) "There is a young married couple in this county, who actually thank God (like unto the over righteous Pharisees of old) that they were born in North Carolina and not in poor Tennessee. They have recently been blessed with a fine boy, and it is proposed that they bestow upon him a name somewhat suggestive of the good old North State, such as Buncombe, or Tar-Heel, or Pitch, or Turpentine"; (2) "When in company with any of the many literary gentlemen of Culleoka, be careful that your words are all properly and chastely pronounced. 'A word to the wise,' & c." A word never to vote for W. R. Webb! Sawney knew he had been libeled as being practically a damyankee, and a blue-nose besides. He never denied being severe on profanity. Now it was unlikely he would ever run in Maury County for anything.

It was true about the baby, though. Sawney and Emma named their firstborn William Robert, Jr. Sawney wrote his family at Oaks he was much relieved that a glint of red he had detected in his baby boy's golden hair was no longer visible. He became the irrepressible proud father, pulling Willie out of his crib at every opportunity to show him off to friends. "All babies are hideous," was the reaction of one middle-aged bachelor preacher. Then after a look at Emma and Sawney's long faces, he added: "Your baby is less hideous than any baby I have seen in some time."

Father and family were in a house along the railroad, on the rise south of the village. Sawney superintended improvements in both "academy" and residence that summer. He also ran a normal school for teachers. In the 1874–1875 school year, the Webbs took in eight student boarders, for a total of fourteen in the two-story residence, including Brother John and relatives of Emma. With five bedrooms and fires to keep up, the household kept everyone very busy, especially Emma.

The view here was beautiful, and their frame house burgeoned with balconies. Sawney thought the prospect was even more beautiful than the one from the mountain field near Stony Point, much as he loved that old boyhood haunt. The hills hereabouts were larger, more rugged, and more broken than around his Carolina home. The trees on the slopes of the bald-topped limestone hills were gorgeous either in the greens of summer or in changing reds and yellows.

Growing Willie toddled eagerly to an east window whenever young boarders living overhead overturned a chair. He mistook the vibration for the passing of the remarkable Iron Horse. The railroad was more than a romantic excitement. It was bringing boys from six states now to the Webbs' little school, although villagers had not yet started any building to replace the moldy basement or the rented room near the saloon, where John was teaching.

The school dramatized a new social style in the South, a disciplined Puritan reaction to the casual, disorderly hell-of-a-fellow life of the rustic antebellum chivalry and post-war stagnation. Students of all sizes—some of them already ordained preachers—pounded crumbly limestone into gravel, then hauled and spread it over Culleoka's dirt roads, which were mud after rains and choking red dust during the summer drouth.

The community grew more prosperous. Sawney's best friend, the big-handed model farmer Claiborne Taylor, set an example for vigorous intelligent work and generous sharing with the less fortunate. Thanks to his large store of corn and his large heart, Taylor Farm during lean years became known as "the land of Egypt." Productive work became fashionable. People lived better. The correspondent to the county weekly repeatedly commented on how few drunks were seen on the village streets, even at Christmas time. Families who sought a more stable environment moved to Culleoka.

"Our patronage is of the best quality and the moral tone of the school is everything we could ask," Sawney wrote his youngest brother Sam. "One boy told me he had not heard an oath since he had been here & that public sentiment among the boys was against it. I have ten young men that will open school with prayer." The honor code became a reality. In four years, eleven students had been educated for the ministry, and ministerial students kept coming, tuition free. Some villagers thought the reaction to casual living was going too far, as a *Herald and Mail* report made plain one holiday season:

Young ladies (God bless their innocent little souls!) were making preparations for a masked party on Christmas night, but alas for the poor girls, their troubles were all for naught—*The Preachers Objected*—And they are so numerous here that it would not be well to oppose them. . . . We all hope the preachers may have no greater sin to answer for in the day when all will be judged according to deeds done in the body. . . .

(Signed) "Hard Times"

The forces of merriment did manage a preacherless, unschooled New Year's comeback. A "grand hop" was held at the hotel in North Culleoka, thanks to proprietor–manager J. T. Bellanfant. A string band made sweet music and "fairy forms" floated in the magic mazes of the dance. North Culleoka became a locus of resistance against community reform. The village divided on the wet-dry issue, and county news reports repeatedly drew attention to the conflict. One village wag acquired a pet rattlesnake to symbolize the "venomous serpent" the "temperance gentlemen" talked about during their indignation meetings. At a victory celebration one night in the early seventies, young Culleoka wets in the wildness of their excitement threw their hats into the bonfire. Then the wag brought out the rattlesnake and his pet raccoon as well, and cast them both alive into the flames.

Rampant paganism did not appeal to Sawney Webb. He was the youngest delegate to a general conference of the Methodist Episcopal Church South which overwhelmingly voted to debar from membership anyone buying, selling, or using alcohol as a beverage. Ratification by three-fourths of the district conferences would have made it Methodist law.

"We have good discipline," Sawney said of the school, "but we had hard work to get it once established. . . . We are obliged every session to cut off some, and this makes enemies that work very hard against us." Sniping articles began appearing in the county news weekly. One alluded to "several cases" of mumps and diphtheria among the students. Another entitled "Cholera in Culleoka" was full of innuendo, adolescent nonsense, and satirical use of Latin and other learned words. The principal of a school twice almost ruined by the fright of deadly disease could not have enjoyed the publicity.

In the fall of 1875, "The Vanderbilt" opened, and Principal John M. Webb went to Nashville for opening exercises. The school's "oldest and best" boys enrolled in the new university.

Another old student returned to Culleoka in late October, after an absence of about eighteen months. Ned Carmack's arrival was like a triumphal homecoming. The school, in fact, was like a home to him. At Christmastime, Ned was the star orator. His speech so impressed Sawney Webb that the schoolmaster could quote from it forty years later. This fatherless youth was someone special to him. The reviewer for the county weekly reported: "Mr. Ned Carmack is full of fun, which becomes contagious even before he makes his bow. . . . The boys say, he is as wise as witty, and I do not doubt it, when he 'gets his smart sayings from Socrates.' " Ned was also one of the four public debaters. He argued with gusto against the proposition that the slanderer is a more pernicious character than the flatterer. Sawney was convinced that Ned was a genius. He watched the youth devour volume after volume of English and classical literature under the wise tutelage of Brother John. He marveled at Ned's sharp wit and rollicking energies.

By 1875 Sawney had grown a beard. It was then somewhat straggly and decidedly red. It did not mask his lingering youthfulness, and nothing hid a look of sadness and profound hurt that sometimes settled in his heavy-lidded eyes. "I feel like a boy," Sawney wrote his own mother in his thirty-third year, "and know that I am not much of a man. . . . When I reflect how good a kind Providence has been to me in giving me such a mother and such brothers and sisters, and such a wife and such children, my heart swells with gratitude." A baby daughter named Alla had been born to Sawney and Emma. "Our little girl is so fat and grows so fast. . . . Everybody says she is very pretty." Fat little Willie "always runs with a glee to the gate to meet me or his Uncle John. . . . I dread raising him among so many boys."

John still boarded with them and was "more of a book worm than ever. I know he is the finest scholar I have ever been associated with and has the clearest head. 'Twould be a poor getalong without him." John shared the title "Principal" on school circulars.

The end of 1875 brought heartening news from The Vanderbilt. Culleoka graduates were the only students who took first honors in the university's first examinations. A flattering rumor became an official fact in January of 1876: "Profs. W. R. and John M. Webb have been offered positions in the Grammar Department of the Vanderbilt University, with good salaries. . . . Don't go, Gentlemen," begged the county newsweekly. They did not go. They preserved their independence and maintained their responsibility. "The value of property in this place depends upon the success of the school," Sawney wrote his mother. "The town has more than trebled since I came here. . . ."

Sawney was happy in his new home. His $250 cistern with a built-in dipper-pipe arrangement gave him running water at his back door—"you never saw any queen's wall that looked nicer inside." He owned a cow and five hogs, and was doing a little vegetable gardening on his large lot, which descended to the south bank of Fountain Creek.

The Vanderbilt offer did revive fund-raising among villagers for the long-promised schoolhouse. Sawney proposed that each student and alumnus plant a remembrance tree on the bare six-acre lot purchased for the campus. At this news, one little boy's soliloquy was overheard in February: "Trees, trees, it's *trees* he wants, a whole grove of them, as if there were not switches enough already here."

In early March, Sawney Webb faced one of the most difficult judicial decisions of his vocational life. The religious-minded boys were holding a revival meeting. A humorless preacher youth with a sepulchral voice and a long-tailed black coat was leading it. Services went poorly. An undertone of irreverence persisted in the student audience.

A counter-revival was merrily rounding up all the unregenerate student "sinners." Sawney Webb knew who the leader of this one must be. Ned Carmack continuously made fun of the young Reverend Joshua, his preacher's "holy" tone, and his solemn manner. Sawney learned to warn his preacher boys and public debaters against affectation. He called Ned in and asked him to stop his "sinners" revival. The young redhead refused. The schoolmaster told him to go home until the end of the revival services. Sawney knew that religious experience could give boys direction and purpose in their lives. Ned was resentful. He considered he was being expelled—or chose to think so. His mother wrote the Webb brothers in March:

I rec'd a letter from Ned this morning bringing to me the sad news of his disgrace. . . . I feel it is due you, as those who would have been friends to my fatherless boy to say something, I scarcely know what. Ned said that you had required him to go home. Poor boy, he has no home, and no money to come to me, and I none to send him. . . . He has always been so thoughtless, and so prone to be led off by evil associations. . . . He has always held you both in such high esteem that I thought you could have more influence over him than anyone else. For a sorrowing mother's sake try him once more if you can.

Fatherless boy. Sorrowing mother. No home. No money. Sawney always said he even offered to pay Ned's expenses while the boy stayed away. He could not allow this brilliant headstrong youth to wag the school. Ned never returned as a student. When Sawney invited him to speak at commencement, he announced that Mr. Webb had educated him by "leading" him "out" the schoolhouse door—in a sardonic allusion to a supposed Latin derivation of the word *educate*. The fatherless youth took a librarian's job in Columbia, later studied for the law, became a brilliant newspaper editor, and rose politically for a time to a position of national prominence. Sawney followed Carmack's career like a doting father. Yet the very kind of behavior that caused Ned's final departure from the school eventually led to an act of violence that ended his life, inflamed the partisan passions of his fellow Tennesseans, aroused indignation throughout the country, and brought Ned's old teacher to the verge of death himself. But that frightful episode was years ahead.

The Culleoka correspondent almost made an issue of young Carmack's departure: "Our young friend . . . has gone to Columbia to live. We miss him muchly." When favorites like Ned leave a small independent school community under such circumstances, friends and followers react with resentment and anger. No school authority figure enjoys popularity at this time. The "Messrs. Webb" were reported shortly afterwards giving a holiday that "permitted the young gentlemen to visit the young ladies." The student body needed a lift without a doubt. Their winsome red-headed funmaker was gone. The thirty-three-year-old schoolmaker gained wisdom from this personally troubling experience.

That fall there was new excitement. The long-awaited academy building was rising on the rocky hillside, just to the northwest across the creek from Sawney's house. The ground plan became a very thick T, with a hump in the middle of a very long eighty-foot crossbar. On several sturdy mortared blocks of limestone, the structure began to rise. The facing was long lath-wide strips of wood fitted horizontally.

Two thirty-foot classrooms flanked the front entrance, and the auditorium, at right angles between, thrust a total of fifty feet toward the rear. A high sloping roof, at the very top, crisscrossed the lower sloping roof of the front "crossbar" and ended at the front itself in the inverted V of the pediment. A dubious decoration sat atop the right side. The two-tiered elongated pyramid, about twenty-five feet high, resembled a half-hearted church steeple. Two high wooden pillars made three generous entrance ways below. About the grounds, big and little students, white-collared in their formal but rumpled suits, posed for photographs. If the painted new facility was not beautiful, it was useful, with 365 feet of blackboard, and the auditorium doubling as a senior room, besides housing the library.

Faculty, students, and friends joyfully walked up the wide steps for the memorable Christmas exercises. A string band that holiday season made the three-room structure vibrate with lively sounds. The debating society cast off the name of Philomathesian, became the Hamilton, and made its academy debut. Dozens of students and villagers signed a pledge to "pave" a lane leading downhill from the academy to the depot. The greatest shortcoming was lack of a campus well.

The villagers who knew that a school is people and not a building were more excited about another event that December. A newspaper correspondent announced with Victorian emphasis: "The union in marriage of a man of intellect, genius, nobility and purity of character, to a woman possessed of the charms of beauty and modesty, together with the corresponding gifts of intelligence and purity of mind, is one of the most important and beautiful events of life."

Shy, gentle John Webb, the object of almost four years of public and private teasing about his bachelorhood, was taking a wife in Nashville. She was the daughter of a Vanderbilt professor. The officiating minister was Bishop McTyeire himself. The Bishop, besides pronouncing them husband and wife, was pronouncing the husband one of the South's best linguists. John's bride was a dainty blonde appropriately named Lily, daughter of Professor and Mrs. Albert Shipp, formerly of Chapel Hill. John's older brother Dick had boarded with them during his antebellum days at the University of North Carolina, and had fallen in love with all the little Shipp children. Villagers felt an unprecedented satisfaction that both brothers were married and content in their new school home.

In the spring of 1877, the schoolmaker completed a fence around the campus, and students organized a second debating society, named the "Platonic." Enrollment was in the eighties. Webb continued to send Vanderbilt the university's outstanding students. They are "always well trained and prepared . . . and . . . generally rise to distinction," according to Chancellor Landon C. Garland. The new university was having great difficulty with youths who demonstrated no love of study, no training of mind, and no knowledge of how to learn. The distractions of the city were too much for them. They were bright enough, but they lacked inner discipline. Vanderbilt now referred poorly prepared students to the Messrs. Webb.

In mid-August, Sawney went to speak before the National Education Association—leaders of schools and colleges from all over America. He took a train to Louisville, Kentucky, enjoying for the first time a Pullman sleeper. The railroads had improved so much that a body would hardly know he was traveling. He woke up early in Louisville, and headed for the NEA meeting place, Leidercratz Hall. Sawney was the only man there when a stranger arrived and asked him the way to a schoolbook publishing house. When Sawney began to give directions by streets, the man blushed in confusion and ignorance. He was from Indian Territory. Sawney walked a mile to show the way. He also handed the grateful stranger his own school circular. Sawney never saw the man again, but he would hear from him.

The schoolmaster turned his mind to the convention. On August 15, he delivered his speech. He called for the independence of secondary schools, for their complete separation from colleges and universities. He pleaded for recognition, long neglected, of high-achieving teachers at the secondary level. He said Vanderbilt's decision not to have its own preparatory department "has brought hope to us all." He insisted that a distinction be maintained between the preparatory school, or high school, and the college or university, the one being adapted to boys, the other to men.

"The college or university is composed of men and governed upon the principles that underlie the government of a well regulated state," Sawney said. "The one-man power here is the most objectionable of all modes of government. . . ." A school is different. "The teacher's authority is delegated by the parent, and he stands in the place of a parent; hence his is necessarily a family government, which by divine appointment is a monarchy. For this family government the number of pupils is necessarily limited. . . . Let the higher institutions of learning foster the preparatory schools, not compete with them." He praised Princeton for having decided to publish the names of schools from which its best scholars came and thus having sent a thrill of joy through the hearts of teachers who had labored with genius for years in relative obscurity.

"The teacher, as an artist, desires to bring before the public specimens of his work," he continued. "The college is the arena for such exposition, or otherwise his merits must be measured by the opinion of his pupils, who oftentimes do not appreciate his labors until long after his working days are over. . . . Frequently the skillful conscientious teacher goes to his last resting-place feeling that his life was a failure."

In conclusion, the Confederate veteran declared: "The military chieftain has his triumphal procession and his laurels; the teacher, who oftentimes exhibits more firmness, persistence, strategy, more gallantry, more real heroism, more genius in his conflict with ignorance and petulance, simply asks recognition at the hands of those who reap the rewards of his victory. . . .' "

It was a strangely prophetic utterance, though little heeded in 1877 from a schoolmaker out of the Tennessee hill country. He never stopped believing a school should be like a home.

IX. Some Toughs—
I Made It Cost Them

Cultivate in a student self-reliance
by teaching him to think
and not merely to accumulate facts—
the accumulation of facts
being desirable only
as furnishing material for thought.
—SAWNEY WEBB

The county weekly reported "a real live Chinaman"
in Maury County. He was baptized Thomas Kelley in honor of his
American sponsor, Methodist minister D. C. Kelley of Nashville.
The young man wanted to study at Vanderbilt and become a missionary to his people. Sawney found his new student's knowledge of
English so rudimentary that he sent him to his sister Susan at Oaks
for intensive tutoring.

Thomas Kelley remained with Sawney's mother and sister
through the winter and early spring of 1877. Then one day he left
them without notice and took the long railroad trip back to Tennessee. They could neither know nor understand male protocol toward women in traditional Chinese culture. They wrote Sawney of
their disappointment and hurt. On May 1, he replied: "Your Chinaman acted badly and I am sorry; but I have had instances of equal

ingratitude on the part of ministers of *our own sort* of people. The
gratitude to be looked for is in the future and *not here.* He will
when he comes to maturity feel kindly towards those who have
helped him."

On that very same day in 1877, Thomas Kelley wrote Sawney's
sister from Nashville:

My Dear teach

"I received your letter in church to night. . . . Your said, in you letter
about your poor mother felt hurt about my leaving your home as I did.
I read the words and I wept about my conduct that give her a trouble.
Now wish you to tell her I will not be so unfeeling no more. . . . I very
much oblige to you had been taught of me.

Susan mailed Thomas Kelley's painful apology to Culleoka, but
added a note: "Sawney, please return this letter to me."

In early November of that same year representatives of another
nation came to study with the Webbs. The correspondent of the
county newspaper professed much excitement: "Indians! Yes, we
have them here. . . . Don't get scared. It isn't . . . Sitting Bull nor
Spotted Tail. . . . [General Custer had made his last stand out west
the year before.] They are of the Choctaw tribe. . . ." Young descendants of aboriginal Americans, those that had survived the infamous "trail of tears" leading from their usurped southeastern
homelands to "Indian territory," were now coming east for a better
education. "Our village school," the *Herald and Mail* correspondent marveled, "has had one Mexican—now of the Vanderbilt, Nashville; one Chinaman, and two Indians. So you see they have had
four distinct races in their school in the last twelve months."

In 1877, Sawney once more became a father. He and Emma
named their second son in honor of his brother John. As his family
grew he tried to build up his personal property as well as the school.
He would always be investing in land. He borrowed money at ten
per cent. "I owed a thousand dollars due one day and when the day
arrived, I couldn't see any way to meet it."

Sawney was hoeing beans when the Chinese youth Thomas Kelley came in great excitement and said there were an Indian chief
and a tribe of Indians at the gate. More Indians! Sawney hurried
down the slope. It was his recollection that there were twenty-three
Choctaw youths with a chief named McCurtain in charge. "I feared
the social effects of housing such a large percentage of my students

Indians," he recalled, "and so I made arrangements to take eight—enough to fill one boarding house. He paid me $225 in green backs for each Indian, making two thousand dollars, the largest sum of money I ever received from one man as school expenses. So after dinner, I called for my thousand dollar note and handed over the green backs as if it were a matter of no moment to me." A letter of introduction presented by Chief McCurtain explained why the Indians came to Culleoka. It was written by the very man from Indian Territory whom Sawney had befriended in Louisville. He had shown Sawney's school circular to McCurtain when the chief and the Indian youths camped on his ranch. Long after the Webb brothers left Culleoka, youths from the Choctaw nation continued to go to school to them.

Sawney wrote his mother: "There is a good deal of prejudice among uneducated men against the Chinaman and the Indians. I hope they will all be useful to their people." Sawney cherished a similar hope for the children of his own blood. He prayed that they might have a life of "usefulness."

John Webb was now a father too. Son Albert was born shortly after the arrival of Sawney's John. Both wife Lily and the baby appeared well in Nashville soon after the birth in September, but days later Albert weighed only five-and-a-quarter pounds. John was a little sensitive about Sawney's "making himself merry" over Albert's size. Baby John was almost four times as heavy. Soon it was obvious that Albert was in a dangerous condition. In the interest of his survival, Sawney's wife Emma agreed to wet-nurse her little nephew-by-marriage. Sawney noted the effect of this arrangement on his own infant children, Alla and John. He wrote his mother: "Sometimes in the small hours of the night we wake up and Alla is by Jno's crib *cooing* and he laughing most heartily. She has never manifested any jealousy of him and resigns her mother's lap in his favor without a protest, although she protests vociferously against Albert's occupying it. He has been nursed by Emma since his arrival in Culleoka and is improving rapidly." Albert not only survived, but learned to talk more quickly than his Cousin John.

The two families had been on intimate terms from the beginning. For months after their marriage, John and Lily boarded with Sawney and Emma. Then they moved into their own frame residence across the iron trestle in the village. They were only "forty-five yards" downhill from the Methodist church by John's own measurement, and a downhill city block from the new schoolhouse. A limestone boulder in John's front yard served for playground equipment as his family grew.

The brothers enjoyed so much patronage now that they feared a "strike" among the boarding house keepers. Students from the village dwindled to a very few. The schoolhouse, however, was becoming a community center, playing host to benefit suppers and holiday celebrations.

The wit of Ned Carmack lingered on, in this published notice with a built-in byline, about goings-on at the Culleoka Institute: "Tongue, ham, oysters, heart, turkey, celery, more tongue, brains, chicken salad, plenty of tongue, more heart, less brains, sausage" etc. . . . Come one, come all—*talking* clerks, *pleading* young lawyers, *killing* young doctors, and handsome *puffing* editors, Sunday School superintendents, expectant politicians, members of the brass band, professional and nonprofessional—and Ned Carmack—who desire patronage, smiles, and votes from the 6th District." All the food a man could eat cost 50 cents, and 25 cents for children under twelve.

In May of 1878, the schoolmaker reported that both scholarship and deportment were the best of his eight years in the village. Only one boy that term needed the rod to convince him that "the way of the transgressor is hard."

In another year, the venerable "Batch" was being built not far from Sawney's house in a field east of the railroad trestle. This rude dormitory for boys of limited means stood on a slight rise just above beautiful Fountain Creek. On the last day of 1879, a nearly grown man named T. Leigh Thompson arrived in a farm wagon. The Webbs made Leigh and two other youths "tenants" of the new bachelors' quarters. Emma sent down hot coffee and sandwiches. The floor was not finished—only half laid—and there were cracks growing between the shrinking green pieces of siding. But the occupants saved money. They brought their food from home—hams, bacon, dried fruits, and even spring chickens dressed for frying. Their cook stove heated the wooden shack in winter. Every morning they walked up the bank of the creek to school. Their "Batch" was also known as "Sycamore Retreat" because of the broad-leaf trees that lined the stream.

The rural poor were always of poignant interest to Sawney Webb. A youth came up to him in the dead of winter in shoes with toes protruding, elbows and knees showing through gaping holes in his clothes. The boy was so lacking in self-respect that he could not speak distinctly. He mumbled, "Got all the boys you want?"

The boy's condition touched Sawney's heart. "I said, 'No, not if you want to come to school.' He said, 'I will come next fall.' He was about 18. I said, 'It must be now or never.' I told him to bring enough rations with him to last a week, and he would go to an old outhouse of my family and eat his cold grub; and what he wore in the schoolhouse for an overcoat was an old blue blanket, and when he came walking up . . . some of the boys began to snicker. . . . When playtime came they asked him who made his overcoat, and I never forgot the boy that went to him and made him his friend. . . . He was just a gentleman. . . . And he made Dan his friend . . . and do you know it wasn't long before the boys gave that young man the position of public debater." The boy in the blue blanket became a leading attorney.

Sawney kept his eye sharp for the youthful hero that practiced a Christian chivalry. No one stirred the teacher's imagination more than Perry Duncan, a boy in knee breeches whose mother taught him the Sermon on the Mount—"and he believed it." Christ had said, "My son, return not evil for evil," and Perry literally turned the other cheek. "When the other boys cuffed him about he didn't resent it and the cowardly little scamps took advantage of him. . . ." Many a time Perry Duncan sat with the schoolmaker in his room to get a little rest from other boys. "I was mean enough to wish that he would get a stick and break it over their heads. And then the landlady took up the torture, and it looked like I was the only protection the boy had. . . ."

There was a pasture downhill from the schoolhouse which faced toward Sawney's own home. Inside the fence was a very dangerous bull. "We had signs stuck up all along the fence to warn strangers not to take the short cut across the pasture," Sawney recalled. "One afternoon just as school was out we were attracted by the screams of a little Negro girl that had got over in the pasture and the bull was charging down on her. . . . I, an old veteran soldier, was transfixed, thinking that I had to see a tragedy . . . without the least hesitation [Perry] laid down his books and leaped the fence and attracted the bull away from the little Negro girl, dodged him like a trained bull fighter till he saw the little girl had got over the fence, then he beat the bull to the fence and got over. . . . I have seen heroic action. In the war I have seen men charge batteries, but I have never seen as

heroic an action as that. . . . Next morning I told the school that
there never was a greater piece of heroism. The boys made that boy
president of his class, president of the school, president of the society. There never was a boy that had influence like that boy—just
because he was heroic."

Sawney perennially campaigned for non-violence in a violent
era in a violent region. He tolerated only two exceptions among his
students. One was the case of two boys who were spoiling to fight
each other. Fight if they will, Sawney declared, but they must go
off into the woods and settle their scores without any witnesses.
Often the extended walk cooled youthful tempers and the pair returned to the schoolyard without a scuffle.

A boy named Wright Flynn was Sawney's own illustration of his
other exception to non-violence. "Wright was a great big boy. He
didn't learn much . . . sat foot of the class. But there were a few other
things about him that . . . I can never forget." One day a bully was
playing leap-frog with some other boys. A "little raw-boned measly
fellow" was down, and instead of jumping over him, the bully took
his knee and knocked the little one winding. "He would not have
knocked a big fellow like that. Wright Flynn said, 'You go with me
to the woods.' He just saved me the trouble," Sawney remembered.

The schoolmaker frequently appointed a young stalwart to give
some big bully or hazer a vigorous beating. He insisted that a bully
was always a coward as well.

Another afternoon, students were making fun of a little village
pauper, who was wearing a man's old coat with its tail dragging the
ground. Wright moved in, took out a piece of paper, and challenged
all boys present to pledge a fund to buy the little boy some decent
clothes. "Wright Flynn . . . I love to honor his memory," Sawney
said.

Sawney's updated Code of Chivalry included a vigorous Gospel
of Do. Students ran their own debating societies, organized their
own sports, explored the countryside, swam in the old millpond a
mile or two down Fountain Creek east of town. He knew the natural freedom he gave was risky. A schoolboy climbing after some
bird's eggs fell from a tree sixty-five feet to the ground. Miracu-
lously, none of his bones were broken, and he returned after a rest
at home, for the next session.

Whirlpools or "sucks" below the dam were so powerful that in
the spring of 1881, a boy was trapped by one, a second boy going to

his rescue was caught in a second suck, and only a Goliath-sized third boy was able to bring the two victims through the narrowest of escapes to safety. Sawney made certain rules for his boys' own good. "No swimming until after the dogwood blooms" was strictly enforced in the spring. Violations took Sawney galloping on his mare Leidy—coat-tails flying—to the scene of a boy's offense against himself. Once a boy died after plunging into icy waters.

As early as 1873, Webb boys had organized a baseball club, which played surrounding towns, and later, the Vanderbilt nine. However, following a defeat by the university team, an incident of sore-headedness and published student accusations against the umpire's honesty caused the schoolmaker to ban all interscholastic athletics. Students played all sorts of sports in meadows and fields—baseball, shinny, football—but games were only intramural.

During the later years at Culleoka, families of both principals grew rapidly. Adeline, Clary, Susan, and little Emma were born to Sawney and Emma, and they stopped taking in student boarders. Daughters Cornelia, Mary, and Sarah were born to John and Lily, and the year of the big move, a second son named Hazel.

In the early 1880s, Lily emphatically endorsed the idea of building separate dormitories for the students, and doing away with the boarding house system. As the two principals discussed the question, Emma carefully refrained from taking a stand. The boarding house system prevailed, but Sawney wrote a letter to his mother, contrasting without comment the approaches Lily and Emma took to their husbands' business.

The two families visited one another often, and the children found it fun to cross the iron trestle that separated the houses, and follow the railroad tracks.

A few years before they all moved away, Sawney contracted tapeworm, a dangerous disease. His son William remembered the strangling effect it had on his father's normally vibrant voice. Sawney consulted three specialists in the East and they all told him nothing could be done. Emma, however, insisted that Sawney let her brother Will Clary come from his home in Bell Buckle to examine him. En route through Nashville by train, Dr. Clary consulted Dr. Paul Eve. He could give no advice, either, but referred Clary to an article on tapeworm in a recent medical journal. Clary read it and wired for medicine immediately. It was male fern. Three days after taking it, Sawney was cured. He had managed to survive again. "When it becomes necessary to move Webb School," he told his family, "I am going to Bell Buckle and put the health of my family into the hands of that country doctor, who knows more than the big specialists of New England."

The greatest problem in Culleoka was beverage alcohol. Some people persisted in selling it to students. One student embezzled $15 of his debating society's dues money to buy liquor for an illegal party. One Thanksgiving holiday, about half a dozen boys took a bottle of liquor out in the woods north of town, behind "Mount Ida," the tallest limestone hill in the vicinity, and drank on the sly for the day.

People were already giving Sawney credit for uncanny powers of intuition when rules of the school were violated. This time he became aware of the hanky panky after sending two secret sinners home by coincidence: their mother was on her deathbed. This development caused a third guilty student to panic and run away. The entire student body was astir.

In morning chapel, Sawney gave an emphatic lecture on "Your Sins Will Find You Out," while Brother John closely scanned all the young faces in the audience. Afterwards, John handed his brother a list of names. The rest was interrogation and expulsion of violaters.

The schoolmaker watched saloon patronage very closely. If he did not approve of the husband of a woman who took in boarders, he did not allow his boys to remain there. Sawney began making bitter enemies. The death of a student was responsible for one of them.

A father wrote from Louisiana, "I have beaten iron eighteen years, in order that I might have an educated son." He sent his boy Albert to the Webbs. Albert seemed to be ailing one day, nothing serious apparently, and he called for a young doctor to come to see him. Sawney recalled that within a day or two as he sat on his front porch, three little boys came running up the long front lot, saying: "Mr. Webb, you must come and see Albert . . . Mr. Webb, you must."

"In the excitement," Sawney recalled, "I knew something was wrong, and I said, 'Is the doctor drunk?' and they said, 'Yes.' I went down there and as I walked in (there was nobody in the room but Albert and the doctor) he pointed to his legs and said, 'My legs are drunk, but my head is all right.' " The doctor did not satisfy Sawney as to what medicine he had given the patient. "I gave a glance at Albert, and I rushed out to get other doctors . . . and as the first doctor that reached the place came walking from the house, I met him at the gate, and he said, 'Albert is dead.' "

Sawney remembered with remorse having to face the bereaved old working father, and the father's searching questions: Was the doctor a good one? Was he the same doctor that Sawney had for his own family? The schoolmaster deprived the doctor of practice among the student boarders. The young man was bitterly resentful. There were reports he made threats on Sawney's life.

The last few years at Culleoka, Sawney would not let his students cross the tracks to the east-side stores because the village saloon was among them. More enemies.

In 1884, he joined a concerted move to invoke a law that was beginning to dry up the state. No liquor sales were to be made within four miles of a chartered school outside an incorporated town. Culleoka was not incorporated then. Attorneys helped him reword the school charter so as to invoke the law in the village. A number of trustees parted company with the Webb School at this time. Some of the wets were dangerous men to oppose. Besides, who was Sawney Webb to deprive a man of his freedom to buy liquor legally if he wanted it? The saloon, in effect, was out of business. More and more enemies.

Sawney took three ways home from school: by the railroad trestle, through a field where the rock-lined creek ran shallow, and across a footbridge he had built for himself. The resentful doctor was reported to lie in ambush. In retrospect, the doctor's own wife was credited with forewarning Sawney how to avoid him. Sawney was shot at when he stepped outside his house at night. Stories are still told of all-night pitched battles in the village community.

Sawney employed a spy named Harlow, a tall middle-aged carpenter and odd-jobs man. People then could not understand why Harlow and his wife seemed to have so much in common with the busy schoolmaster. Later their role became known and the Harlows lost some friends in the village.

Porter Warner, later a Chattanooga industrialist, was eyewitness and student participant in one fracas. Dressing for church one Sunday morning, Warner and his boarding house mates looked out and saw a gang of men waiting for Sawney as he crossed his footbridge. "About the time he hit the side of the bank, one of the B—— boys stepped up and knocked him down. All of us boys went down there to give old Sawney a helping hand, but by the time we reached the bank of the creek, Old Sawney had gotten up and knocked B—— down and was on top of him, and B—— was scratching and trying to get loose."

About a dozen boys stood by to be certain Sawney received a fair fight. "Old Sawney finally let him up and as soon as B—— got on his feet, he up and slapped Old Sawney on the side of the head, and then a bunch of us boys knocked B—— down and pounded his teeth out." The schoolmaker himself said of the incident, "I would have been killed by those men right there, but the schoolboys came and rescued me."

Another Sunday, Sawney was headed for his afternoon lecture in the schoolhouse, when a gang met him and knocked him down. This time students were again watching. A number of them, led by Tom Lytle, ran down the hill, grabbing palings off old Billy Wilkes's fence, and drove the men off. Sawney had to restrain his boys to keep them from doing violence on his attackers, according to village contemporaries.

During his last year at Culleoka, the town voted on the issue of incorporation. Male citizens who missed the convenience of buying their liquor locally and legally, gave incorporation the victory. Chartered school or none, an incorporated town could have its saloon. No women, then, of course, were entitled to vote. By the fall of 1885, Sawney was negotiating a move with Dr. Clary and other leading citizens of Bell Buckle.

At Christmastime, some exuberant young "wets" overreached themselves in their celebration of victory. In the twilight of December 25, the school conformed to a longtime custom of setting off fireworks. Students divided into groups to shoot Roman candles, launch skyrockets, and toss about fiery balls of cotton soaked in turpentine. The rocky hillside schoolyard was a spectacle of lights that fateful 1885. Suddenly, "Company Q" arrived. A girl student remembered: "I was busy shooting my Roman candles, looked around. The place was deserted, fires were out, fireworks kicked around . . . everybody was running." A young man from North Carolina, Sawney and John's nephew William A. Webb, remembered being kicked by one of the intruders. Son Will, then about eleven, was tending chutes for skyrockets when a member of Company Q came up. "Oh, N——, don't destroy that," Will remembered pleading. The invader swung his axe at the boy. The "toughs" wrecked about $54 worth of fireworks, according to Sawney. With controlled fury, he took the riotous young men (of good families) to court in Columbia, subpoenaed everybody involved as witnesses, and placed the entire student body and faculty on the train.

Four hell-raisers were found guilty of profanity and were fined five dollars and costs. Two pleaded guilty to assault and battery and paid twenty dollars and costs each. Other assault charges against the four were scheduled for the spring session at the county courthouse. Sixty dollars was not excessive. The "costs" were otherwise. Every witness received an allowance of ten cents a mile, to and from Columbia, plus a dollar a day. "I made it cost them about $1,500," Sawney said.

In February he was back home at Oaks. Certainly his life was never in greater danger. Possibly he was recuperating from a severe beating that, according to tradition, he received from his enemies. After a brief triumphal return to Culleoka, in which students cheered him lustily at the depot, he went over to Bell Buckle to superintend construction of school buildings. Brother John ran the school in his absence, and Sawney told their mother it was better run than if he had been at the schoolhouse.

By May, the lingering assault charges against "Company Q" were dropped. Within less than a month the Webbs were gone.

There is a vivid account of the move: "The first Culleoka knew of Webb's intentions was seeing two mule teams, loaded with boys and baggage, disappearing into the distance. . . . In this all-day cross-country jaunt of some forty-odd miles, the students went through their usual study and recitation periods, while bumping along, sitting on loose planks across open farm wagons. Of course, each boy had been warned to pack for an early start the next day and threatened to keep quiet about it. This whole episode certainly is unique among the annals of the teaching profession. . . ." This alleged move is, in fact, so "unique" that it never happened. A Bell Buckle graduate of a dozen years later wrote it in a memoir, and some people still retell the story and believe it to be true.

The Webbs' intention to move was no secret that spring. It was reported in the newspapers, even in Nashville. Old Sawney did not do his moving "on the sly."

In 1886 both Webbs did become residents of the railroad village where a "country doctor" who had cured Sawney of the tapeworm was practicing his profession. Twenty years of struggle after the land-shattering Civil War, the schoolmaker found his permanent home.

X. The Bell Buckle
Declaration of Independence

A successful school
brings business prosperity
and often gathers around it
a population of selfish people
who look upon the school
from a purely financial standpoint,
just as the world looks upon
a creamery or a packinghouse.
—SAWNEY WEBB

Commencement 1886 lacked entertainment. Few visitors were in the audience. There were no youthful declamations, no public debate. The students' chief interest was in watching Old Sawney declare the Webb School's independence. On Wednesday, May 26, the Webbs were taking public and official leave of the steepled schoolhouse in Culleoka.

The schoolmaker was never livelier. He cut a stocky figure in his frocktail coat, for he had put on weight in sixteen years. The scrawny look was gone. His beard had filled out into a neat red spade. The wounded look of the past did not show in his gray-blue eyes. They could still look gentle, but they could also look frighteningly fierce. Sawney's very nose had lost the upturned lilt of his youth and had taken on a sturdy Roman shape. His dry tenor voice would not be heard again on this rocky hillside for thirty-five years, and then under the most improbable of circumstances. The boys believed it would be never.

He was standing at the lectern, facing the rows of half-filled wooden benches. Senior Elliston (Monk) Farrell remembered all his life that the schoolmaker penetrated the expectant silence with these emphatic words: ". . . And now it becomes my painful duty to announce the closing of this school. The forces of evil have triumphed in the recent election. My brother and I do not feel that a boy's school can serve its purpose in a rum-ridden environment. Local option has made this town wet; the Webbs exercise their option to leave the town *high* and *dry*. We move our school thirty-five miles eastward, to Bell Buckle, Tennessee."

Up went a piercing, overwhelming Rebel yell—"YI PEEEEEEE! SAWNEY!" Students were shouting the ineluctable nickname to his face. To them, he had already become *Old* Sawney, although he was only forty-four years of age. His own fatherhood was legend now. Villagers were already gossiping in Bell Buckle, before the move, that Sawney Webb knew everything that went on in his school. Only a young Culleoka alumnus turned schoolmaster was so rash as to suggest to the villagers that Old Sawney was not literally omniscient. And for having opened his mouth on the subject, he felt compelled afterwards to write his old teacher a letter of apology.

Somebody told the Nashville newspapers that the brevity of Commencement 1886 was due to the need "to let the boys from a distance reach their homes before the time for the change of gauge by the railroads." This evidence of progress was a happy coincidence. Thousands of miles of southern track were being relaid to a standard 4 feet 8½ inches to conform to tracks throughout the rest of the country. Rapid transit was drawing the technologically backward South more firmly into the national Union. Sawney regarded the move to Bell Buckle as progress, too.

A thoughtless world regarded a school as a building. It was really an association of men and ideas. "Brick and mortar do not make a school, nor can they," said Sawney Webb. Men and books and portable equipment—those were a proper and practical investment. A school should never invest in "immovable real estate." If a community or neighborhood in its "greed" made the environment undesirable, the human beings with their books and portable equipment could exercise their portability and move elsewhere. "A neighboring community, for the sake of the prosperity, will furnish the plant necessary and, from the collapse of the business of the former location, will co-operate with the faculty to minimize the evils of environment." Sawney wrote it all down several years later for the Methodists in a pamphlet on "The Value and Dignity of Secondary Schools."

But these principles were his Bell Buckle Declaration of Independence. This is the way it was brought to fulfillment: A joint stock company of leading Bell Buckle citizens raised $12,000—a small fortune in those days. There were also six acres for a campus, which A. D. Fugitt turned over to the board of trustees for a fraction of their established value. The Webbs could use the money virtually as they saw fit.

A legal technicality forced them to leave the library at Culleoka behind. So they decided to put two-thirds of the money—a total of $8,000—into books, and scholarly John Webb did the choosing. They invested only $400 in a building to hold the books, and the new schoolhouse itself cost only $2,200. Far more than $12,000 was at stake in the village, as Sawney knew. The school was stirring up a boomlet.

New houses had gone up that spring. Bustling little Bell Buckle kept all its own "mechanics" busy, and employed the mechanics of neighboring communities. Parents with children to educate and would-be boardinghouse keepers, some of them from Culleoka, bought or rented all the empty houses. Local business men reported that others could be rented "if capitalists would invest in building."

Bell Buckle was fifty miles southeast of Nashville on the railroad tracks to Chattanooga. On the west side of "Railroad Square" the brick freight depot with a 100-foot-long stockyard and a cattle chute explained the community's economic origins. Farther west of the tracks were other business houses facing the railroad, including Jeff Davis's two-story red-brick saloon. Still farther west was the creek, which local wags said the Bell Buckle bartender used to stretch his profits.

East was the "right side" of the tracks, with a large cluster of brick stores. A white-painted pillared hotel in Southern mansion style stood across a street behind the passenger depot. Graveled Main Street, at right angles to the "square," led a visitor east up the hill, past several more brick stores on the left. Off to the right was a little spring where a perishable artifact had given the village its unusual name.

The concave outlines of a cow bell and a buckle once appeared on the smooth gray bark of an ancient beech tree beside a little run-off from the spring. A Cherokee Indian carved this pictograph, according to local historians. It signified that white men were violating a treaty which limited them to lands six miles north of Bell Buckle Spring. A cow with a white man's bell buckled around her neck had apparently wandered that far south of the line. In 1852, the railroad located its first depot about a hundred yards east of the locally famous tree. The main interest of 1886, however, was the six acres of beautiful beech forest set in blue grass about one-third of a mile east of the depot. That summer, the hilltop campus became "a pleasant resort of Sunday afternoons" for the young people. A 103½-foot well was dug. At last, "abundant" water was handy.

Just east of the well, an honest, sturdy piece of architecture was rising. It was much like the old Culleoka schoolhouse, but bigger and better and without the dubious steeple. Yet it was about as basic a structure as one could imagine without calling it a barn. Some people thought its 30-foot-high arched entrance made it look like a livery stable. Everybody would soon be calling it "The Big Room."

The ground plan resembled nothing so much as a wide-winged, snub-nosed, twin-engine jet—although such a shape, like the school itself, was ahead of its time. The only "brick and mortar" were the chimney-wide square foundations, which held the new wooden building off the ground. Wing to wing, the front was about 125 feet long, with four high and narrow windows showing on either side, and a total of ten light-giving windows in each of the 40 x 25-foot side classrooms. On the trailing edge of each wing were little 12 x 12 cloakrooms with windows. The boys' name for them was "whipping rooms" because of their sometime function. Chalked graffiti like "Hit him one for me, sir"—never obscenity—would eventually appear on their wooden walls. Huge sliding doors connected the ninth- and tenth-grade wings to the auditorium. It stretched to 70 feet in length, behind the "cavernous" entrance. The floor of the auditorium sloped upwards toward the rear, and the platform stood down front, against a wall just behind the entrance and vestibule.

Raising the high peaked roof caused difficulty. The "mechanics" balked, they thought it would collapse. However, as in the case of his rearranged Confederate coat after the war, Sawney's own knowledge of geometry assured him otherwise, and he won his point. He

was proud that the high peaked roof was competely free of support-
ing pillars inside the assembly hall. He would have no posts block-
ing a boy's view of the platform or of him, or his own view of an
inattentive young rascal.

There were a couple of other peak-roofed wooden school buildings, each about 25 x 35 feet in size. The Senior Room sat in the
northwest corner of the campus, with the exciting new library at
one end. A twin Junior Room sat southeast of the Big Room. All
buildings were faced with horizontal wooden strips snugly fitted together. All were painted a kind of battleship gray. All the rooms
were heated with pot-bellied stoves, and were often freezing cold in
winter. A two-story box house also went up that summer on Webb
family property near where the brothers were building: two rooms
above, two rooms below, with an outdoor kitchen. It was named
"Thompson Hall," for the first occupant of the Culleoka "Batch."
It would save young men of limited means a good fifty per cent on
room and board. They could employ a cook and tend a pea patch
and obtain other eatables on Sawney's new farm.

Although school was late in starting that August, the Big Room
was not quite finished. The place had the exciting smell of fresh
lumber as the students arrived on their new campus. Chaos always
seemed to be the rule on opening days—unorganized boys noisily
milling about, up and down the steps of the schoolhouse, chasing
around the schoolyard and village, shouting joyous "hellos" to old
friends and tentatively making new ones. Opening day in 1886 was
especially noisy—the student body had never been so large. Old
Sawney, however, was determined to start promptly at one and he
was exasperated when his quick eye caught several new boys steal-
ing into assembly, a little late, around the new platform.

"What do you mean coming in here behind time?" he demanded.

"Our dinner was late, sir," one new boy remembered stammering.

"You didn't come here to eat!"

However, the old master communicated deep concern as well as
impatience: In a few days, with an eye on the landlady in question,
he came and took a look into those boys' dinner basket, and found
only a cold, dry, uncut young chicken and some little knotty biscuits. The little boys went out of that landlady's house, and into a
less mercenary home environment.

Community resistance to Old Sawney's will was best personified by a trustee who insisted on turning his cattle into the schoolyard for grazing. Trustees held the "immovable real estate." Sawney had not found time to build a stile and fence around the campus—yet. He told the trustee, however, that he must not graze cattle there. Sawney would not have his schoolboys running and playing in filth. The trustee said he would graze his cattle there when he pleased. Sawney warned him if he did, his boys would scatter the cattle all over the countryside. The willful old trustee put his livestock on the campus anyway. The next morning they were gone. Sawney's eldest son recalled that the owner had to hunt all over Bedford County to round them up.

The same local citizen also ordered Sawney to give up Bingham's *Latin Grammar* in favor of another. Give up the work of his old teacher, the late brilliant and beloved William Bingham? Sawney had carefully stipulated that the immovable real estate was the trustees' only concern, and that they had no voice in running the school. He told the villager to mind his own business. The local trustee threatened to cut Old Sawney out of the society of Bell Buckle if he did not use another book. Sawney's reply was the nearest he was ever known to have come to using profanity: "Cut and bedogged!" he said.

This was the era in which his legend grew as a man virtually unsurpassed for his insight into boy nature. Before Gilbert and Sullivan's *Mikado* boasted of making punishments fit the crime, Old Sawney had been learning to bring wit and humor into school discipline.

"Lawrence Nichols," the redbeard intoned in his intense tenor voice from the platform, "Come back Saturday morning. You were shooting marbles out of bounds and in study hours." On Saturday, in the northwest corner of the schoolyard, while a teacher sat in the library reading, the miscreant was bidden to "ring 'em up" and shoot by himself under the window for about three hours.

This incident was a forerunner of his most famous case: a carriage maker's son who persisted in playing hookey to go fishing. One Friday morning the schoolmaster directed another student to show the defiant little fisherman the rain-barrel just outside the Big Room, then sentenced the offender to fish all Saturday long in the barrel with a piece of string and a bent pin.

In those days, Sawney taught the tenth grade (Caesar) class, and this meant "trapping," the Webb School importation from Sister

Suny's and Old Bingham's. Trapping was a kind of spelling bee in very rapid motion. As many as a hundred boys would sit on the edge of their rough oaken benches in the usual semicircle. As one former student recalled it, "A boldly put question; a poor answer; 'Next.' A correct answer, or probably a deluge of 'Next! Next! Next!' Finally 'Take him,' and he 'took him,' which means that Jim trapped Sam or many 'Sams.' "

Jim would move just ahead of the first boy who answered the question wrong, and the several losers would slide foot along the benches. A student who reached "head" and held that position for a day would receive a "distinction," remove himself to "foot," and attempt to move head again for another distinction. The game was competitive, rapid-fire, and most exacting. Little boys wore the benches smooth with the seats of their corduroy pants in the stress of anticipating a chance to answer. Some became so excited that they would ease off their benches, crouching on air, hands raised and waving. "I had never been up against just such a scramble as that one," an alumnus said, "a scramble I maintain worth seeing, worth being part of, for did it not mean zeal, competition, but, above all, accuracy?"

Trapping did not instill love of learning for its own sake, of course; but then, the unadorned fundamentals of an intellectual discipline do not really do so, ever. Of what use are forms and lists of vocabulary words—or algebraic equations—to the inchoate intellect of a fourteen-year-old? Sawney as a driller did teach his boys to love excellence and to take pride in accuracy, without which all higher learning is limited and any genuine mastery impossible. Under such tutelage a hitherto neglected young will and intellect would quicken. Boys who had difficulties in their early years at Bell Buckle would excel in their upper-school years and even go on to take honors in college.

"After an hour of firing questions," an old boy would remember, "Old Sawney's feet getting higher on the chair in front of him and his bow tie retreating further and further and further toward the occipital region, with many interspersed 'Nexts,' 'Take him,' and 'My, my, my's,' the class was dispersed." How sarcastic the "My, my, my's" could seem! One husky boy from Arkansas, smarting under the teacher's tongue-lashing, complained that Latin was just too hard for him.

Sawney returned: "Too hard, eh? Want something easy? What

about all the people who have gone before you learning Latin? Come with me." The old tactician got up, put on his wide-brimmed hat, and paced the derelict down to the book store. He called for a McGuffey's *Third Reader,* led the boy back, and gave him a special seat on the platform. "There, you want to study something you already know." The second day the embarrassed boy begged off. Before the end of the term, springing up from his seat on the roots of an old beech tree, he ran without his hat about a quarter of a mile to Old Sawney's house, rang the bell, and beamed when the old master appeared: "Mr. Webb, I just had to come and tell you, now the confounded stuff makes sense."

In the summer of 1887, the schoolmaker had moved his family into their massive, two-story frame residence. From there he ruled *in loco parentis* over the school, over boarding houses that stretched from mid-village a mile or so out the pikes, and by influence over the village itself. A student remembered it as "all one kingdom, one family." It was anything but perfect. It was very human. It was effective.

That fall, Old Sawney came to school and announced that a little boy had arrived in town who could speak Greek as well as he could speak English. His gray-blue eyes hinted mischief and some of the students guessed before he told them: his eighth, and last, child had been born. Sawney and Emma gave the name Richard Thompson to this second-generation schoolmaker of the future.

Sawney continued a practice with his growing children which he had begun with Will and Alla at Culleoka, teaching them their primary three R's himself. It was a struggle for this constitutionally impatient, driving man to cope with the first mental gropings of little children, yet he did it with unusual empathy. Once he was reading the story of King Midas to his son Clary, and the little boy burst into tears when the avaricious king's daughter Marigold turned to cold metal. Father Sawney immediately broke out crying, too, and schoolboys walked past that morning in wonderment at the bearded man and his little son sobbing out their hearts.

The father was enthusiastic about his new farm as an ideal environment for raising his boys in the Bingham tradition. One day he told son William to go out into the field, rope a half-grown calf, and bring it to the barnyard near the house. Sawney said that if man was made to have dominion over the cattle, a boy ought to have dominion over a calf. The little blond-headed boy doggedly went out, roped the youthful animal. He tugged and fought. It took him all afternoon, but he managed to pull the balky calf into the vicinity of the barn. Both boy and animal were exhausted. William looked expectantly at his father. Sawney said he did not have any special reason for having the calf brought in, but he wanted to find out whether Will had the spunk and force to do the job.

In the summer of 1889 he was determined to take William to Europe. His years of "worrying with boys" had become professional routine, and he dreaded the evil effects of unrelieved monotony. He always loved to see industrial fairs and expositions, and this year Paris was playing hostess to World Progress, and unveiling her famous new landmark, the Eiffel Tower. Two Culleoka alumni joined the W. R. Webbs, Senior and Junior: The Reverend George L. Beale, a portly young man now teaching at Bell Buckle, and W. H. Witt, who was studying to be a physician.

The party toured the shrines and landmarks of English literature. Ellen's Island, made famous in Scott's "Lady of the Lake," was on the itinerary at Will's request. A little Scottish steamer took them out in the Loch, but because it made no stop at Ellen's, Sawney decided to rent a rowboat. They rowed for miles and, in spite of very cold rain, they stayed on the island long enough to gather ivy. After the seemingly endless return, the four were drenched, chilled through, and aching tired. They were so bedraggled that they were not even allowed to enter the kitchen of the one resort hotel. Prohibitionist Sawney Webb decided this was an emergency. He bought a bottle of brandy, and measured out spoonfuls, like medicine, to the group. Minister Beale, alone, would not touch it.

As they walked, they found a peasant hut. The rain had subsided, and a Scottish woman was washing outdoors. She invited them in to share her peat fire, and would not take a penny for her hospitality. As fifteen-year-old Will grew warm, his tongue thickened. Under the influence of the brandy, he talked in such garbled language that the woman said in bewilderment, "I dinna ken. I dinna ken." Old boys Witt and Beale took a look at Will's father's face. They had never seen their old teacher so scandalized, or mortified. For them it was probably the most hilarious incident of their travels.

Old Sawney himself preferred to remember his visit to Eton. A proctor showed the visiting Americans around the famous school. So people insisted on making fun of the Bell Buckle schoolbuildings? The seats, desks, and even the Big Room were "better" than the ones at this great old institution. "Millionaire aristocrats in

England," Sawney said, "want their boys to learn to stand hardship. There isn't a church at Bell Buckle that isn't better than the church at Eton where Edward VII went to church."

Old Sawney, Will remembered, was curious about other things at Eton.

"If I should leave my son here, what would it cost, sir?" the American schoolmaster asked.

"Are you a gentleman, sir?"

"In my country, everyone is assumed to be a gentleman, unless he proves otherwise, sir."

Appearances, appearances. Sawney noticed that every cab driver he saw in London was better dressed than any member of his party.

They traveled to Paris, visited the Louvre, and ran into a relative from North Carolina who tried to straighten Sawney's black string tie. They joined the excitement on Bastille Day, July 14, when the Tower was opened to the public. Sawney was amazed at "so many people, soldiers, shahs, and sheiks." He had never seen such throngs.

There was political trouble. As they passed a government house, tables and benches began flying in different directions on the street, and gendarmes were grabbing first one man and then another. The overflow of human beings came close to panicking. Sawney firmly grasped his son and took him behind an iron lamp post. The old expert in human survival explained that the post would prevent their being run down and crushed.

They saw many Catholic priests in their dark frocks, and once in a train compartment Sawney conversed at length with a French cleric, each man expressing himself in written Latin, for their systems of pronounciation were different. Thus the onetime international language remained sufficiently alive to serve its function between a European priest and a teacher from the hills of Tennessee.

Sawney, however, was getting fretful. Mail from home was not reaching them. He was miserably homesick. Finally, they heard that Brother John, left in charge of the school that summer, had suffered a nervous breakdown, and had gone to a sanitarium. Sawney almost panicked, regretted ever having neglected the school for this jaunt in Europe, cut short their planned tour of Holland and arranged to sail home as soon as possible. "This school in my heart is next after my home," he used to tell his students. Both home and school were too far away.

On his return, his wife and assistant Grier Peoples explained: Emma had handled the business with Grier's assistance, enrolled more than two hundred students, and hired one new teacher. "I thought I was needed. I find I'm not," Sawney remarked. He learned to pay other tributes to his wife. No one knew better than she what an eccentric character she had for a husband. Late that fall he demonstrated the scattered and careless style that became part of the Old Sawney legend.

On frequent occasions, he would without announcement or fanfare pull off the train a governor, senator, bishop, successful farmer, businessman, preacher, or college don from Vanderbilt—gentlemen whose character Sawney knew and approved—and at once provide his boys with living examples of the "large life" he stressed in his morning talks.

On a visit to Nashville in late November, he invited Vanderbilt Professor W. M. Baskervill to come to Bell Buckle on a Saturday night to give the boys a lecture on Sunday afternoon. Baskervill accepted, but "as usual," Sawney's niece wrote Sawney's mother, he forgot to tell his wife about the invitation. When the Saturday evening came, he had forgotten it himself. However, after Emma and the children were off to bed, he made his customary walk south on Maple Avenue and west on Main Street to the night train. He nearly always met the trains to pick up his mail or the latest newspaper. Not once did he think of Baskervill until the professor appeared on the depot platform. Sawney's memory jogged him. He stepped up to the professor as if he had come especially to greet him, took him home, showed him into the guest chamber, and went to bed without a word to Emma.

The next morning Sawney did not awake until the bell was ringing for breakfast. As he was drawing on his boots he remembered. "Emma," he said, "Dr. Baskervill is in the guest chamber. I invited him two weeks ago." Her hazel eyes panicked. She rushed down to reset the table and give out another breakfast to be cooked, came back, and changed her own dress and those of all the children. Relaxing a little, she looked around at her husband. He was wearing the most disreputable-looking suit of clothes he owned. He was a very stubborn man. Emma won this particular contest over the amenities by influencing Sawney to change to a better suit. But it was an endless battle with her independent-minded patriarch, and she fought it lovingly. He admitted, years later, that she spent her married life "trying to civilize me."

XI. Let the Boy Understand It Is a Game

When you are an old man,
I want you to remember
that your old teacher said,
"Don't ever be a spectator;
take a hand in the game."
—SAWNEY WEBB

He was practicing the most mysterious, difficult, dangerous, controversial, and misunderstood of all the arts. His medium was the live growing material of the human spirit. "The will power is the man," he said. His experience proved it. "It is not what we can teach you but the principles we can inspire you with."

He knew that the best practice of an art is a form of play. "Let the boy understand it is a game," he told a group of student teachers. He repeatedly offered a barrel of apples to a boy who could put anything over on him. "If you come here to have fun at my expense, I will have some at your expense," he told new students. He brought vigor, zest, and humor to his game of wills with the young. "To come in contact with human wills is not pleasant," was his understated warning to anyone daring to attempt it.

"All sorts of building men do," he said, "is done on lines of least resistance except building character. That is done on lines of greatest resistance." And he, Sawney Webb, was the *force de resistance*.

109

For him, cold indifference, impersonal neglect, and social isolation were far more demoralizing—and cruel—than tongue-lashing, dispassionate switching on the palm of the hand, or making fun of an obstinate boy's folly. Nothing made a youth feel so worthless, or so sick with despair, as to find that little or nothing was expected of him. It was madness not to offer high-powered young people some great ideal to live up to. "I have no hope for a boy's future," he said, "if he is not filled with a profound reverence for somebody, or something."

Old Sawney's game was remarkably Zen-like in its character. He found abundant lessons in nature. He relied on spontaneous moves, abrupt confrontations, and rough surprises. When thoughtless little boys went astray like sheep, he might choose to discipline them in a herd, but he knew that "mass education" is a contradiction in terms. "I never try to treat two cases alike," he said. "When two boys are caught at the same offense and are treated differently, I never try to explain except to the parents. They have a right to know." To explain it to the boys would have been as tedious as trying to explain a joke.

Human living was a strenuous game of multiple choices. His "sons" were trying them all. The infinite variables of human nature put his game beyond the certainties of any so-called science. Since his game was the practice of an art, everybody enjoyed the victory if anybody did. Likewise, if the boy lost, the teacher failed, too. "My son, if I can't help you I will send you home. I'll not take your father's money for nothing." There were other schools, other teachers, other opportunities.

His role was Father. So he lost no time in personally confronting a new "son." "My office is out under these trees. I don't stay in the house any more than I can help," he told opening-day assembly. Then he marched out to the shade of his favorite beech, sat down in his cane-bottom hickory chair, and tilted himself at a considerable angle against the great gray trunk.

He was a homespun psychologist, a Puritan Socrates with a southern accent, a curiously powerful personality, this compact, quick, broadshouldered man in a wide-brimmed hat, with a quid of tobacco swelling his bearded cheek. He could not care less that his black string tie rode his stiff white collar at a crazy angle, that his vest was partly unbuttoned or misbuttoned, or that his frocktail coat and pants appeared too rumpled to have submitted to one of

Emma's conscientious pressings. If a new boy quaking before him noticed anything at first, he most likely would have seen the schoolmaker's wrinkled black shoes, with the square toes and high laces, riding the rung of his tilted chair.

Eventually the student found himself in the grasp of two spirited blue eyes, intently measuring, examining, searching, challenging. The stare could chill a boy's spine. Perhaps for the first time, he found himself being treated not as a child but as a human equal. "You are no longer a baby," he made this announcement from the Big Room platform. "You are now thrown on your own resources. Your parents can't make a man of you. Your teachers can't. I want you to realize the responsibility is on your own shoulders, and that this is the right time to make a start—this session."

At that first interview, however, he only *looked* it and never *said* it in words.

"Study Latin at Wallace's?" he might ask.

"Yes, sir."

"What grammar did you use?"

"Bennett's *Latin Grammar.*"

"You are assigned to Caesar." Then some personal talk, perhaps, that surprised the boy with how much the man knew about him. "Caesar" meant the tenth grade. If the new boy had simply answered, "Why sir, it was a little brown book," he would have been placed in Beginners, among the little ninth graders.

"We make mistakes," he said. "Oh yes! I never expect to stop making them." He challenged every boy to *prove* how big a mistake he had made.

"I want the teachers to watch," he announced on the second day. "First I want them to look for the boy that can be promoted. Don't look for the boy that has to be turned back this morning. Let's look for the boy that has to be promoted. . . . A boy in a new environment is always embarrassed, and doesn't do himself justice. . . . If he can be promoted, there isn't anything that would give us more pleasure."

But he had a fierce prejudice against a boy who sounded too glibly sure of himself. "I have started a boy in our Senior Class by mistake. . . . He told me he had read Sallust, Cicero, Caesar, and so on, and I said, 'I am glad, my boy.' He dropped from class to class and when he finally landed foot in the Beginner Class, he was very much depressed. I was depressed. He came around to see me and he said, 'Mr. Webb, you have made a very great mistake in regard to my character.' I said, 'I haven't made any charge.' He said, 'I want to tell you something about myself. I never took a chew of tobacco in my life. I have never smoked. I have never taken a drink of liquor. I've never told a lie in my life.' I said, 'I accept your statement. But a pair of breeches stuffed with sawdust never took a chew of tobacco, nor smoked, nor took a drink of liquor, nor told a lie.' "

The boys in the Big Room laughed at the story. The old man meant no flippancy. "I wanted to quicken that boy's spirit. He was a negative.

"But my son, listen to me, there is a positive nature for *you* this morning. . . . My son, listen, I'll tell you the kind of boy I like. I like the fellow that if he were to see the White House or St. Paul's or St. Peter's would say, 'I couldn't build anything like that now but I can learn it.' When I see a boy take his knife and cut his top; when I see him mutilate his father's residence; that boy is a savage. The very minute I see him get a knife and make him a baseball bat, fix him up a racket, and take pains in constructing, I know that civilization has begun to work in him. In your uncivilized condition you would cut your fingers and toes off if it didn't hurt."

Character is an *educated* will.

He sent savages home as quickly as he could. His school was not equipped to handle them. One fall he told his faculty they must watch out for a new boy he had taken the measure of—never to turn their back on him—for he was dangerous. Yet one teacher did turn his back within a few days and the boy stuck a knife in the man. The vicious boy was shipped immediately, but colleagues remembered that Old Sawney was more outdone with the wounded teacher for not having taken warning.

He was grateful that youthful manners grew gentler as the violent era withdrew into history. Yet resistance to his vigorous methods flared occasionally and brought the game of wills very close to a state of war.

A lad that had been whipped on the hands came pointing a shotgun at Sawney, vowing to kill him. The teacher leveled his formidable eyes on the eyes of the anger-crazed youth: "Go ahead and shoot. Of course you will hang for it. Don't keep me in suspense—shoot." The muzzle of the gun began to weave circles. Just as the barrel swung out of his face, Sawney pushed it and instantly disarmed his would-be killer.

Even in the late 1890s, a boastful bully was goaded into making threats. He stood up in class one morning and, according to an eyewitness, told Sawney Webb, "You can't talk to me like that, I won't take it." "In a maximum of 10 or 20 seconds," the eyewitness reported, "and hard to see from my distance of ten feet, Sawney had him on his back on the floor, and was calmly placing his chair over him, with the lowest rung almost touching his neck. Seating himself in the chair, Sawney continued to the end of the class, apparently unconscious of the boy beneath it. At the close of class the boy . . . was taken out, whipped, and expelled." The narrator was amazed. Sawney was fifty-five years of age at the time, and his youthful adversary was a husky 180 pounds. It was the teacher's will that carried the decisive weight.

Old Sawney knew that expulsion was his last chance to salvage a particular game from defeat and failure. He sternly warned an unruly boy that he was sure to come to a bad end, that he would land in the penitentiary in less than five years, that he would not be the first ex-student to do so. Sometimes this seemed the only way to jolt a headstrong youth into thoughts of maturity. When the boy eventually achieved eminence, Old Sawney could not have been more delighted. If "his boy" still held a grudge, it simply was too bad he had not outgrown his adolescence. How gratifying, Sawney felt, that his personality had been powerful enough to ride that boy's wild will, like a bearded superego with coat-tails flying, through the years.

Many non-graduates of Old Sawney's discipline were proud to call themselves alumni of Webb.

The youth who showed no spirit may have troubled Sawney more than a wild one. "I saw a boy try to ride a horse. The first time the horse bucked up just a little bit he dropped his bridle rein and humped up on the horse. The horse understood and he just bucked a little, and that fellow flew off. That fellow was a weakling. . . . God gave you a spinal column. Have more backbone than a fishing worm, my son." Old Sawney despised the cult of the easy. He pushed the timid boy into preparing a speech and delivering it before the big audience of Commencement Week.

"I wouldn't see the other fellow play," he said. "I would either get in the game or I would go away and not look at it. . . . I wouldn't stay out on the piazza and look through the window at the other fellow talking to the girl. . . . I wouldn't play second fiddle to any man. . . . To me the most distressing thing in college life is the athletics. Four or five hundred fellows let eleven get the development, but how about the others?"

On the weekend holiday at Bell Buckle—Saturday during the earlier days, and Monday later—he urged every boy to meditate, though he would never have used such a high-fallutin word.

"Now why give Saturday? . . . I believe that every boy ought to have a day in which to know himself—in order that he may learn himself. . . . Go off by yourself and plan your life, taking no one's advice but that inner conscience which dictates to us all if we listen, and tells us right from wrong. . . . My life is limited by what I know. . . . The little baby starts in with a piece of information. He knows where his grub is and he knows when he's hungry. That's the size of his life. But that body will develop and grow and he can ride a stick horse. If he is an idiot he will never get any further than that. . . . If he is endowed with a mind he will pick up additional information. . . . Just in proportion as you get information is the size of your life. . . .

"You may get millions of dollars. That don't cut any figure. I am sorry for the poor millionaire that don't know how to enjoy himself. I have seen them. . . . Dollars are tools and they are good tools. So is a horse rake and a horse mower. . . . Dollars are tools to make exchange with . . . and the man that ignores them is as big a fool as the man that ignores the axe and the saw. Now I want you to get the idea that the man is bigger than the tool—the horse rake, the horse mower. Yes, the man is bigger than the locomotive, the grandest *thing* you ever saw or ever will see, perhaps. . . . Boys, I want a man. That's the reason I make these talks. . . . Wisdom is the principal thing. Exalt her. Make her the big thing. 'She shall promote thee.' "

A school should be rough and stimulating enough to make a boy want to grow up and leave it as soon as possible. "There was a boy I examined yesterday. . . . I believe if I can get him to recite lessons to me or some other teacher, I can save him a year and let him get married a year sooner. . . ."

The veteran marched up and down, his coat-tails tossing into the air in tandem to his decisive stride, carrying a book steadily on his head to show how "General Lee" taught him to walk, and warning his boys to avoid the sauntering "scrub strut." Or he stood with thumbs in his pockets and his stocky fingers in spread eagle, the square toes of his shoes poking over the edge of the stage. Or he presided nervously behind the dark-stained lectern where his Bible lay, pounding the wood for emphasis with his nearly numb right arm.

He challenged the boys to cite a human situation or predicament that did not have some parallel in a Bible story.

"What about a boy going off to boarding school, Mr. Webb?" one boy was reported to have asked.

"That's easy," Sawney is said to have replied. "Shadrach, Meshach, Abednego, and Daniel—and boys, for once they made the complaint that the food at boarding school wasn't plain enough! Daniel was first honor man, so pronounced by the examining board in Babylon . . . Daniel arose to be prime minister. . . ."

A proud young Civil War buff complained he could not learn mathematics. Sawney opened the text, pointed to the credentials of the author, and told the boy: "You take that old book, my son, shake your finger at it, and say: 'Professor Wentworth, you doggone old Yankee, there's nothing you can put on these pages that I can't learn!' "

A junior was certain that Greek was impossible for him. Old Sawney invited the boy to take a walk. They arrived at a boarding house where a parrot had listened to another student reciting Greek verb forms every morning before breakfast. The parrot did what parrots are famous for, and the boy took a fresh approach to learning Greek.

Old Sawney changed his tactics when he saw boys overdoing their studies. The son of a landlady weighed only sixty-seven pounds at the end of his Caesar year, was reading all the time, and not growing. He advised her to remove the boy from school for several months and encourage him to go out hunting every day. The boy responded to the treatment. He grew to a vigorous manhood, and was leading an active business life at the age of ninety.

Sawney's eldest son Will went stale in his senior year. He barely passed at Christmas time, and said he wanted to stop school. The father looked tenderly at his son, and said, "William, if you don't want to go to school, you don't have to." He told the youth to pack all his clothes. "We're going to get you a job." Will was off to farmer Alfred Barnes's. He plowed from daylight to dark. After a month of farm labor, he asked to return to school. "Son, if I want you to quit before you're 21, I'll tell you, but don't you mention it," Sawney said. Will was only sixteen then.

Late the following summer he called his son back home. "Willie," Old Sawney said, "I've made the greatest possible mistake in your education. You've had too much of me. . . . I'm going to send you as far away as I can—you're going to Phillips Andover." He had searched New England for the best possible school, and decided on the academy in Massachusetts because of its outstanding teachers.

While Will was away at Andover, his favorite dog, a shaggy-haired survivor of the Culleoka days, came to a bad end. Old Sawney broke the unhappy news in the form of a fable:

My dear Son,
Old Carlo was killed last night, and, son, I'm afraid he wasn't the good dog we always thought he was. I don't know how he fooled us so, but he must have been a sneak all along. Last night dogs killed eight of Mr. Skeen's sheep. Mr. Skeen and Sawson managed to shoot four of the dogs, Carlo in the number. I wouldn't believe it until I drove out there and saw him with my own eyes. There is no mistake.

He was so old and stiff that I don't see how he traveled so far. He didn't have a single tooth and I could find no wool or blood in his mouth. I am sure Carlo was killed because he was in bad company. And he didn't have to do it.

Several times in the night, I heard Sandy and Shep barking and if Carlo had only staid with them, he would be living now. What a pity he didn't know how 'blessed is the dog, that walketh not in the counsel of the ungodly,' or that 'the wages of sin is death' for dogs as well as men. . . .

Later, Son Will himself produced an impressive live animal teaching aid after his return from the University of North Carolina. His fine-blooded registered cow stood contentedly as she was milked so long as he squeezed her teats in balanced fashion on both sides of her udder, but when human fingers pulled from one side only, she gave a kick. One afternoon Will was tutoring a weak student in Latin as he milked, and the cow kicked whenever the boy missed. The next afternoon a crowd was on hand to watch the act!

Will teamed up with his father in one of their greatest challenges: a game with a clever boy out of control, whose talent for chaos had not yet grown vicious. Their artful opponent was little Harry Applebaum, of incorrigible reputation, from Mississippi. On his first appearance, around the turn of the century, he extorted a nickel from his father by starting to jump up and down in

a mud puddle just before their visit to Old Sawney. Harry was classi-
fied a Beginner, and assigned to Son Will's class.

The boy's first notable act of mischief was to frolic across the
village west of the tracks and push some little children into the
creek. Next he failed to show up for school and was located dis-
rupting communications by pulling wires out of the village switch-
board as fast as the telephone operator could plug them in. A few
days later, Harry again failed to show up for morning roll call. The
Webbs thought he had run away. Messengers reported the con-
trary: Harry had run west through the square, across the railroad,
over the creek bridge, and up the hill to the public school, where
an elderly retired missionary was the teacher. Harry had danced into
the schoolroom, to the giggles and guffaws of the children there,
and the entire body of pupils were out of control. Sawney told his
son to go and get Harry. When Will arrived, he saw the old missionary on his knees praying for deliverance. Standing beside the
old teacher, passing his thin arms in a gesture of blessing above the
bowed gray head, was Harry, smiling benignly. Old Sawney con-
ferred with his son afterward. "William, don't let anybody know
that you know what happened. Harry was a success today, and you
can't fight a success. But since Harry *was* a success, he'll repeat in a
few days, and then is the time for us to go into action."

Four days later, Harry was absent from school again. This time,
Old Sawney went for Harry. When the man entered the public
school building, the boy jumped up and ran out the back door.
Harry slipped into Bob Paty's barn and hid, but Old Sawney was
right behind. He entered the barn. A piping little voice broke the
stillness. Harry was tired of Mr. Webb's old school and he was
not going there any more. The disciplinarian glanced around the
gloomy interior, close with the heavy smells of animals and harness: "Harry, when I deal with a stubborn mule, I put a halter on
him." Sawney reached up, grabbed a halter rope, and decisively
approached the only boy he ever tied. Crosswise the boy's hands
hung in an instant.

Taking the other end of the halter, Sawney marched the flushed
child back down Clary Hill, across the creek, through the village
square, and up Main Street toward the schoolyard. At the sight of
the Big Room Harry vainly pleaded compromise. Into Beginners
Latin class the schoolmaster marched his captive, and ignoring the

suppressed merriment of Harry's colleagues, whispered to Will: "Don't turn this boy loose until you've conquered him."

Classes ended, and the "dinner" hour began. Will untied one of Harry's hands, and sat behind him in the Big Room as the boy ate from the sack his landlady had supplied him. Harry had little appetite. Then Son Will crossed the road with his captive to the new two-story Will Webb house, the big one with the stained glass window in the chimney. There he tied Harry to a newell post and went inside to eat. Will had little appetite too. Back to school they went for afternoon class, Harry's hands still haltered.

When school was out, they crossed the gravel street again to Will's garden, where Harry soon found himself tied to a fence post. As Will Webb worked his vegetables, Harry kicked clods of earth into the air in a vain effort to break holes in Will's greenhouse down in the hollow. The hours passed in silence. Supper for the two was much the same as lunch. Then Will led Harry off to night school, a study hall for students without self-discipline. When they came to the stile, Harry broke the silence. His tone was grumpy and his look sulky. What was Mr. Webb going to do with him tonight?

"Lock you up in the closet."

What was Mr. Webb going to do with him tomorrow?

"I'm going to put this rope back on you."

Harry's tense little face softened and he asked in a gentle tone: Couldn't they talk this over?

Will Webb never recalled giving a more sincere reply: "Why certainly, Harry, I'd be glad to talk it over."

They sat down together on the wide wooden stile. The boy promised that if Mr. Webb would remove the rope, he would never give any more trouble. When the rope came off his hands, Harry actually tried to kiss his teacher. Afterwards, schoolmates recalled, Harry followed Old Sawney around like a favorite grandson. And why not? This man had given him moral security.

Decades, half a century, or even as many as eighty years after their individual experiences of Old Sawney, a chorus of old boys sang their various memories:

"He made you want to do things."

"Knew how to get more out of boys than any other man I've ever known."

"I took a dim view of moralizing discourse, and have taken forty years to recover. But I see very clearly *now* that no boy ever for a moment could think that his personal character and potential integrity was of no interest to the older generation. Sawney 'communicated' in spite of boys' indifference."

Another old boy remembered "the kindness which shone in Sawney's eyes—and he looked at me when he talked to me—as he undertook to develop manliness and character in me."

Some thought otherwise, one declaring: "The plain truth is that, in addition to . . . remarkable merits . . . Mr. W. R. (Sawney) Webb was vain, boastful, garrulous, browbeating, domineering, despotic, tyrannical, and arrogant, arrogant, arrogant. . . ."

"You either liked him very much or he repelled you very much," was an understatement. Some individuals undoubtedly suffered from an overdose of his personality.

Growing up is never comfortable, and the man who assists the process will always offend. "Oh, my boy," the old eccentric said cheerfully, "you may call me an egotist if you want to, but I'm willing to be called anything if I can influence you to be better. . . . I hope it can be done pleasantly."

XII. You Possibly Have Heard This Is a Reform School

You have got to put restrictions
on your tastes and your appetites
or you will never accomplish
the purpose that you have in view.
—SAWNEY WEBB

No school bell rang at Bell Buckle. A pocket watch, healthy lungs, and a simple ritual took its place. Every schoolday morning, Old Sawney emerged from his gabled castle of cream yellow, and marched south two blocks on Maple to the northeast corner of Main. There he and Old Johnny and three or four assistants held a quick faculty meeting. Boys were already in the schoolyard, out of their Spartan quarters early. Webb and Company soon came marching up the hill, Old Sawney in the lead. "Comin'!" some boy cried, and scores of young coyote voices made it a chorus. At this signal, the several girls whom Sawney never failed to have among the student body, demurely hitched their long skirts and ran for the stile, ahead of the teachers.

The old leader struck the bottom step, holding his timepiece in his hand. He mounted the stile and was careful to cross it on the exact second of 8:30 A.M. "Over!" the boys shouted, and the faculty arrived. Only then did the boys on "exile" cross the stile, rushing furiously. These violators of school ground rules had to hurry. Every boy was expected to be inside and seated by the time the faculty had marched down the gravel path and entered the Big Room.

"Comin'!" . . . "Over!" . . . Seated. The origin of the ritual remains a mystery although it was practiced in the Culleoka days and it resembled the ancient "Faculty!" cry at Horner's.

There was a tedious calling of the roll. Some boys involuntarily memorized parts of it for life. Sawney read a passage from an old Bible. He loomed behind the massive dark-stained lectern. Members of his own large but intimate family circle remembered him as half a foot taller than his actual five feet eight inches. He stepped out and gave a brief prayer on his knees. Every boy was to be on his "prayer bones." "If you are conscientious on that subject come to see me privately," Sawney said. "The posture of the body is a very suggestive thing. It suggests ideals and thoughts. . . ." Next he would speak five minutes or ten minutes, sometimes longer. When a serious problem arose in the school, he might occasionally speak for two hours, or even all day, if the case was really a bad one. Recitation periods were similarly flexible. Every schoolday was different. On an average of about once a month, when the lessons and the weather were right, he would rise from his knees and say, "You may have the day," and two hundred deliriously happy boys would erupt.

The whooping and hollering of surprise holidays reached every house in Bell Buckle. Boys in dark corduroys tumbled out of the high narrow windows. They pressed around the front platform through the doorways, and leaped the steps under the high archway. Back inside, female students from the village pulled their long skirts aside to avoid the male stampede. "You can't ever feel the freedom we had," one old boy remembered for half a century.

On a warm day, students roamed the fields. They went on picnics. They climbed Old Baldy northeast of the village. They crawled into the dark limestone caves. In winter, boys and girls ice skated on Thach Pond east of the schoolyard, or coasted on sleds down snow-covered Clary Hill. The slant of the slope was a delicious challenge: to ride the western edge of the creek bank without an accident. Frequently, a young scoundrel rolled off his sled just in time to let his pretty passenger tumble into the water. Many a laughing girl ran shivering home in drenched clothes that were already stiffening in the freezing weather.

On most mornings, however, there were lectures. Old Sawney had the moral crust to invade the twentieth century with an updated Code of Chivalry—and boys remained or left, depending on whether or not they could live with it. School rules were relatively few and simple. The ethical standards made it difficult. "I can't take time to say that you mustn't throw biscuits at the landlady's head," the schoolmaker said. "When a man makes an excuse for a fool by saying boys will be boys, he makes me sick, and I say, 'Gentlemen will be gentlemen, too.' "

He despised uniformity. "God made you different. I wouldn't try to be like other people, have hair cut like somebody else or wear clothes like somebody else. . . . Don't be a me-too. . . . You can afford to be criticized—that don't amount to a row of pins—but for heaven's sake, I want to say, for God's sake, don't be a *sneak*. Don't connect yourself with a thing that has to be hidden . . . going out into the shadows of night . . . 35 or 60 men going out against one man, and taking him out and hanging him. . . . There are so many thousands of things . . . that can be settled by this little rule: *Don't do things on the sly.* . . . My son . . . *nothing* on the sly! I never was guilty of espionage in my life. If I can't find out your meanness without peeping through the windows, it will never be found out! . . . We treat you as a gentleman. . . . Sometimes it is a violent supposition."

The old man's eyes usually seemed to be scanning the ceiling, but he noticed the slightest disturbance—like inattention one morning at the farthest distance from the stage. "The boys on the two back benches, come forward." A roomful of necks turned east, and as many as three hundred eyes focused on the culprits. They hesitated. "Come on forward—come right to the front." Down the aisle they poked with embarrassment—smirks or sullenness or shame on their red faces—and with genuine fear. "Here's room. Come right up close to me." They settled down on front benches and looked up at him, so near they could see the pale gray-blue pupils of his penetrating eyes. "Some of these days you boys that were brought forward from the back seat will be so thankful that you came in contact with a man that wouldn't allow you to treat him with discourtesy. . . ." One "old boy" remembered seeing Old Sawney bound from the platform and knock the heads of two inattentive boys together.

Yet he knew how to plead for a sensitive consideration of others. "I had a poor fellow working for me the other day when the news came that Dr. Freeman was dead. That man told me that his wife was sick one night, but Dr. Freeman got up and went out, got his horse. He was sick, but he went out and spent the night when he knew he wouldn't get a cent for it. I would like to live like that. . . . Boys, I believe in the sacredness of human life. . . . You may call me an arrant coward; but I'll run every time before I'll kill a man . . . I wouldn't kill even a snake. If his life is any pleasure to him, let him have it."

His notions of reverence led him to take a curiously severe attitude toward profanity. It was grounds for immediate expulsion. "I was on a train one time. The fellows of those days cursed. They have quit it now. A fellow undertook to tell a story and every two or three sentences he had in his damn and goddamn and so on. When he got through I said I wanted to tell a story.

"I said: 'I saw a fellow get in a fight with another one and, shovel-and-tongs, he drew back and he took him right on the nose, and shovel-and-tongs—if he didn't knock his nose off!' People looked . . . and wondered what in the world shovel-and-tongs had to do with it. . . . I said: 'I went to school, but I couldn't learn any language to express myself.' You ought to have seen the smile that went over those faces. God, deliver me from the language of the tough! . . . I sent away twenty-five boys in one day for profanity."

He overreached himself. Every few years he came before the seniors, asked each one whether he had used profanity or not, and required a yes-or-no answer. If a boy answered yes, he was told to pack his things and leave. One boy would have missed graduation if his alumnus-father had not been able to persuade Old Sawney to give the boy another chance. This same boy avoided playing football that year so as not to risk uttering another oath.

A Mississippi Rhodes scholar, who did not enjoy his student days at Bell Buckle, said years later: "The Webb School was the only place I have ever known where nobody would tell a lie. There wasn't one boy in that school who would lie. I've never seen anything like it." No classroom, not even the library, was ever locked.

"Now," Sawney said on the first day of term examinations, "you have had more liberties in this school than in any other you were ever in. My son, you must not speak to another person inside of these grounds today. If you want a knife or a pencil or anything, you ask your teacher to get it for you. Your papers will not be taken before twelve o'clock. They will not be taken then if they are not neat and clean. We can't base civilization on filth."

Every boy signed his name to the following: "I pledge on my honor as a gentleman that I have neither given nor received aid on this examination." "Don't break your pledge. There are no adjectives in it so no lawyer can turn or twist it," the boys were told. After writing examinations on the blackboard, teachers often left the schoolroom, especially in the junior and senior year. As one old boy said sixty years after graduation, "Through the influence of Old Sawney there was in that school the highest sense of honor I have ever known anywhere in my life. . . . Boys themselves would invite a violator to go home."

Gambling was another forbidden pastime. Boys that bet even small change on athletic contests were subject to expulsion.

Sawney regarded the "commercial spirit" as an enemy. He deplored the insincerity of the "commercial smirk" in the place of a genuine smile. "The Material Age: It distresses me," he said. He was appalled by the things that an obsessive lust for profit poked at the mouths of people of all ages. He had reason to exercise extreme caution in dealing with chemical novelties that, as he said, aimed for "your nickels." He had survived packaged and bottled invitations to human disaster long before the federal Pure Food and Drug restrictions. He despised all enterprise that preyed on human weakness.

He was especially hostile to cigarettes. Many a bright, liberated young mind of his day believed this attitude to be extremely silly. He said he banned cigarettes because of a respected doctor's diagnosis. A student was suffering from symptoms of epilepsy, and Old Sawney sought medical advice. "I heard as great a physician as Dr. Atkinson in Nashville say it was caused by smoking cigarettes. Then I said: 'A boy shan't stay here and smoke cigarettes.' . . . The only concession we are going to make, you may smoke pipes and cigars in your room. . . . It is a great pity that you smoke at all. I cultivated a taste for tobacco when I was a soldier. It isn't nice; it makes me ashamed. I can't chew in church and I seldom go into a ladies' parlor where I can't chew and the lady tries to entertain me and my mind is on a chew of tobacco that I can't take. . . ." And the boys that learned to hate him liked to bait his memory, especially in his old age, with the brown tobacco juice that might stain the front of his shirt. And boys that always revered him might recall his attempts to pop a small piece of tobacco into his mouth, almost on the sly, and remember how it once bounced off his cheek and went rattling across the wooden floor.

No man ever tried harder to be honest with the younger generation. No man ever gave their sharp eyes and critical faculties more comprehensive adult material to practice on. The most dramatic danger he feared for his boys was "the ropers," assorted confidence men, swindlers, gamblers, petty thieves, panhandlers, and prostitutes that lurked in railroad stations of cities to catch callow or unwary travelers. "Son, the ropers are out to catch you; it is a terrible thing to be caught by them."

He told the story of a boy who had to be removed from school because of syphilis. The parents said their son was with a large crowd of boys who spent the night in Chattanooga, and some of the bigger boys persuaded him to go to a brothel. His contraction of the virtually incurable disease "spoiled his life." Another life broken off at the beginning. . . .

Sawney gave graphic instructions how to handle a roper. With a flick of his coattails, he strode into the slightest suggestion of a crouch, put his thumb to his nose, wiggled his four fingers, and shouted: "Yaaaaaaaannnnnnh!" Little boys practiced this technique with great enjoyment.

The village square was out of bounds except for errands, the railroad station included. "I don't want you to get acquainted with the loafers. . . . Our study hours begin at supper time and continue to 12 o'clock the next day with the privilege of eating and sleeping all you can. . . . I will never raise any disturbance with the boy who goes to sleep. . . . But . . . the boarding house is no place for games." A boy pledged his honor not to be absent from his premises at night. "At twelve o'clock we have two hours [dinnertime] . . . an hour and a half recitation in the afternoon and the rest play time. And we will be very glad if you will play—every boy in school . . . and we put no restriction upon our games. . . ."

A boy also pledged his "honor as a gentleman" not to keep firearms in his possession—pistols being expressly forbidden in unhappy memory of the Violent Era. A boy could, however, bring his shotgun and use it on holidays. "Now I don't want a fellow to look at a book tomorrow afternoon," Sawney sometimes announced on Friday. "Go to my jungle and hunt. There are over seven hundred acres and you are welcome to hunt over every foot of it." This was property he acquired six miles east of town. Too often careless boys shot farmers' livestock. Once a group was responsible for the death of a neighbor's valuable imported horse. Old Sawney appointed a panel of student jurors to hear the case, and their unanimous verdict was that the offenders be permanently denied the hunting privilege.

In the schoolyard each class took charge of its own special grounds during class time and study hours. No trespassing by a member of any other class was permitted. One boy known to have "put one over" on Old Sawney was a handicapped student who broke this rule. James Frazer Stokes was charged with having stepped on the Caesar grounds when he was only a Beginner. Sawney asked Jimmy at assembly whether he was guilty.

"Yes, Mr. Webb, I did put one foot over on the other ground."

Sawney replied that the "offending foot" could spend three hours at Saturday school. Jimmy had lost a leg when he was twelve, and was wearing an artificial limb. So when he reported to Saturday School he left the detachable leg inside and went out to play with the other boys, propelling himself on crutches. Sawney accepted in good nature this real-life version of a vaudeville gag and permitted the unserved sentence to be laughed off. He never quarreled with a unique success.

There were a couple of other ground rules: "You mustn't touch these trees. We have raised all these trees . . . except these old beech trees. If boys pull the leaves off we couldn't raise them. . . . I hope we will have a yard with plenty of shade for the future generation." A boy who so much as pulled a leaf off a tree was expected to turn himself in and plant a sapling on the school grounds as penance.

My son, do something that will be an aid to those that follow after us. . . .

"This yard is the picnic grounds for the people for a hundred miles. I am mighty glad to have attractive grounds so that they love to come here." If a boy climbed the wire fence, he was obligated to construct a simple two-step stile on the spot of his misdemeanor. Pairs of well-planted stakes stood facing each other across the fence at frequent intervals, especially along the north side of the schoolyard paralleling Main Street. Balls often flew out of the playing area in the heat of a contest. Sawney believed in stiles, for he insisted no school full of boys could ever learn to close a gate.

Boarding houses varied. Some motherly landladies corresponded with their old boys for a lifetime. The best cooks served up hot biscuits, richly flavored country ham, chicken, and beef in mouthwatering plenty. At most houses food was plain but generally abundant, though one old boy complained of having received meat only once a day, and nothing at night but two large pans of butterless biscuits and muffins, plus a pitcher of sorghum molasses.

The chief discomforts actually arose from life in Spartan quarters: two boys in a double bed, small coal stoves with a small pipe through the ceiling, or a fireplace. Baths were an especial rigor. A galvanized tub was filled from cistern or pump, with no more than a heated tea kettle full of water to remove the chill in winter. It was no wonder Old Sawney talked so frequently about breaking ice to take his Civil War baths. In later years the school built a bathhouse to encourage reluctant boys. The schoolmaker did not neglect one earthy detail of a boy's life. He talked about the itch, the unhygienic boy who smelled, and other crude things that shocked the tender ears of children being brought up in the Genteel Tradition.

In their crowded rooms, the boys studied. Sly games, horseplay and roughhouse developed, in spite of good intentions, and in such cases a peremptory knock on the door could be terrifying. Each house usually had one or two seniors to help keep order, and teachers had access to boys' quarters any time of the day or night. A student caught neglecting his studies was forced to go to "night school." One old boy remembered having to walk from his boarding house through the black section of Bell Buckle before crossing the tracks and continuing east up the hill to that night study hall. "All the Negro homes sat on foundations about two feet off the ground—and under each and every one of those houses were two or three hound dogs. What a fuss those dogs set up as I walked in the middle of the dusty road in the dark. I felt like Daniel walking through the Lions' Den. . . . I believe those hound dogs taught me more Latin than I would ever have learned without them."

But switching was the greatest of all discomforts, though relatively few students ever received it. Old Sawney was sure it quickened the spirit of some apathetic scholars. One remembered trying to toughen his palms by every method known: "We tried soaking our hands in alum—in vinegar—and placing rosin on our hands—

but I never was able to find any cure for it except by having the lesson prepared."

Even in the hardier days many a boy that started at Webb did not care to live long under its rigors and ordeals. If a boy in the judgment of the principals pursued a course of "factious opposition" or took pleasure in "making himself disagreeable," the principals reserved the right to remove the boy from school without specific charge. It is not surprising, then, that a Beginner Class of eighty-odd students shrank to twenty or less by the start of senior year.

"Be a man," Sawney cried, "and be able to stand hardship and bad food and cold and hunger and even Old Sawney Webb, and if you can write your mother and tell her how you can stand all these things you'll make a bird sing in her heart. . . ." Or he would declare in a ringing tone of menace, "They know you. You have made a failure at home. You have made a failure wherever you were put." Then, softly, "Now, my son, let me plead with you. . . ."

The boy with whom Sawney's pleas were effective, who responded to the challenges and lived up to the Webb Code of Chivalry, did not become a knight or necessarily mount a horse. However, he did become a chair-man. When he was sure of staying, he went down to a village store and bought a status symbol of his own that cost at one time no more than fifty cents: an unfinished canebottom chair. He carved his initials on it, carried it about like his books, and sat in it proudly outdoors, indoors, everywhere.

What was the formidable old schoolmaker's secret in dealing with boys, in spite of methods pronounced severe even in his own times? Perhaps he answered the question himself in a letter to his own first teacher, just after he had spent the day at his "Jungle Farm," coping with mules and cows that were among his flock of lambs. "I felt indebted to you," he told Sister Susan, "for strength of body enough to chase wild hogs over steep rugged hills. You know *I am* past 62 years of age. I am still a boy with a boy's feelings. When people treat me with deference, I am embarrassed. I feel still the boyish reverence myself." He retained the sensitive feelings of a boy. "I never write a letter to parents, telling of misconduct, after dinner. It excites me so I can't sleep that night. . . . I always do it early in the morning so that the day's work may quiet my nervous system. . . . It is the most painful thing that I ever had to do." Nevertheless, he lived up to his exacting principles, and stood by his teachers. He refused to indulge the dangerous fantasies of those parents who find that their children can do no wrong. To a mother who insisted her son had never told her a lie in his life, Old Sawney was reported to have remarked, "*My* mother was smart enough to catch *me* at it."

Once when an influential bishop insisted that Sawney fire one of his teachers, he expelled the bishop's son instead. Some fathers became so angry that they came to Bell Buckle to fight him. One grandfather threatened him in the manner of the oldtime southern chivalry. Sawney had written him that his grandson had been caught in a lie. The grandfather replied in words like these: "No man has ever called a M—— a liar and lived. I'll be in Bell Buckle next Thursday afternoon on the 4:30 train and we will settle this." Sawney reacted immediately. His letter went like this:

Dear Colonel M——,

I was a Confederate soldier for four years and during that time I got tired of fighting. Since then, I have employed a man to do my fighting for me.

He will be at the station when you get off the train next Thursday afternoon. You can recognize him by his blue uniform, his brass buttons, and his club.

The Colonel did not arrive.

Sawney made full-grown enemies, he imposed hard rules, he gave all kinds of boys a chance, he handled them at their most ungovernable age, and he could be a terror to the unruly. He lived with a violent heritage in a country historically known for a lax and permissive attitude toward youth. No wonder he could say with understatement, "You possibly have heard that this is a reform school." He believed in training. Yet "good boys" were supposed to need no "training."

Sometimes it seemed as if people of all ages slandered the Webb School—and hated him. "I am glad that you can work under discouragements," he wrote his youngest son in 1907. " 'Blues' is man's normal state, it seems to me. I have been in the midst of it all my life and have worked with not only 'blues,' but with the active opposition of kinfolks and neighbors. . . . I have not tried to be anybody but myself. I longed for approval—but from neighbors and kinfolks I have had but little. Be yourself, with God's approval."

Underneath the tough hide of his indomitable will lived the lonely spirit of the shy Oaks farm boy.

XIII. The More Subtle Influence of Gentle John

You must go to sources
to find what man really thought and believed;
you cannot take the labels of men.
—JOHN WEBB

Old Johnny avoided speeches. He never published. He gave no orders. He entered no controversies. He might quietly appear—a slightly bowed and bearded figure—in the doorway of the $400 classroom and library, and look out among the trees.

"Books," he always said. Or he would sit inside reading, and say, "Books," hardly raising his voice. The word would move the seniors to their feet as if at a sharp command.

Older youths in their open shirts and dark corduroys and a few girls in their puffed-sleeve dresses would approach the peak-roofed box of a building. They had arrived at a modest residence of high civilization. Some thought of it as an entrance to the Elysian Fields.

Sawney once asked a senior, "When you were a Beginner here, you thought seniors were little gods, didn't you?"

"Yes sir, I did," the youth replied.

"Well, what do you think now?"

"I still think they are, sir," the boy replied.

It is unlikely that his face carried even the suggestion of a smile. He was one of Old Johnny's at last. He had put away childish things.

He had earned the privilege to enter the sanctuary of the scholar. The younger brother directed classroom drama in a subtle key. The conflicts were an inspired wrestling with perfection, quiet struggles with the Ideal. He was a senior's confidant and adviser, his very close friend. He met a spiritual need of boys in their late teens. Many reverently remembered him as John the Beloved.

He always began class by asking a simple question. If a recitation fell far short of competence the gentle man with the strange bump of wisdom on his forehead would turn his long face sadly away with the muted cry: "It's enough to make the angels weep." The vision on which his mild blue eyes sometimes seemed to rest gave students the intimation that he was well acquainted with the angels.

Even a slight rebuke from him could be a traumatic experience. One morning a senior girl from the village gave a particularly lame answer to one of his questions. "Oh, how can you say that," he said. She fainted.

"It would just break your heart to have Mr. Webb disappointed in you," a senior boy said without embarrassment or shame. Another admitted, "I'd rather have a whipping from Old Sawney than have Mr. John laugh at me."

One day his gentle challenges met one disappointing response after another. At last he was silent. He understood the instructive power of silences. He untilted his splitbottom chair, slowly arose to his feet, and faced the high-paned window toward the west. The seniors turned their heads and saw tears running down Old Johnny's cheeks. He took out a handkerchief and wiped his eyes. "Class dismissed," he said. As they were leaving in shame, "Please do better tomorrow," he begged softly. The next day everyone was letter perfect.

"Old Johnny learned so much that he had to have an annex made to his head," was the kind of remark lower classmen made about his wisdom bump. It was the first thing a boy noticed about him as he sat on the platform in the Big Room behind his militant brother. The knob in the middle of John's high forehead was about a quarter of a dollar in size. Some observers likened it to an embedded walnut. It was, in fact, an emblem of brute violence. The horn of a cow had struck him on the forehead, and the wound had hardened. No man could have lived during wartime and reconstruction and abhorred all forms of violence more than he. There was a tradition that the only time he whipped a boy he cried his eyes out. In the earliest Bell Buckle days, while Old Sawney was away, he had whipped a boy for killing a cow with a shotgun. The boy himself told a schoolmate that the gentle brother wept as he administered punishment.

The tensions and strife of the anxious latter days of Culleoka were deeply disturbing to John. His wife Lily felt that the extra responsibilities he took there during the months of Sawney's absence had permanently affected his nerves. During the first year at Bell Buckle, he became ill. A couple of years later, he lost his winsome baby son Hazel, and the stricken father and sympathetic uncle named Bell Buckle's cemetery in memory of the little boy.

John Webb's finely attuned nature gave him an empathy for pain in the lowliest creatures. He set traps to catch the moles that threw up chains of destructive mounds all over his blue-grass lawn. However, when he heard the snap of the deadly device, he rushed out in anguish. "Poor little fellow! Poor little fellow!" he exclaimed.

He suffered strange phobias and tiny antipathies. Deeply versed in the culture of Europe, he never went there because, it was said, he could not abide the sight of an apparently endless expanse of water. He could not tolerate a daughter's wearing a dress with stripes. He could not bear to listen to "Couldn't Hear Nobody Pray" because he had once heard a Negro singing the old spiritual in a jail at midnight. Attacks of depression came upon him, especially in the spring. His older brother took him traveling in the mountains when his spirits were extremely low.

Once he became ill at Christmastime, when there were but four teachers for 230 boys, an extraordinarily large school. Old Johnny sent word by Ed Baird, who lived at his house, that the seniors should do what they could. The class, acting in committee, unanimously agreed that in addition to their regular daily stint in Latin and German, they should finish the remaining three books of Xenophon's *Anabasis*—in Greek, of course.

When after four weeks, he returned to the little gray-painted house on the edge of the campus, he began at the head of the class: "Ed Baird, how much Xenophon have you read?"

"Finished the fourth book, sir."

"What's that you say?"

"Finished the fourth book, sir."

"Ed Bullock?"

"Finished the fourth book, sir."

The same answer came from twenty-four other seniors.

"We'll see," he said.

Every difficult construction, every irregular Greek verb, every tricky noun or adjective, every passage whose interpretation required skill and polish, became a probe, a trial, a challenge. However, not for nothing had these twenty-six seniors pooled their knowledge, searched grammar and dictionaries, and drilled one another in the senior room, under the trees, and in their boardinghouses. "We didn't go home to dinner at noon despite the ringing of the alarm clock—unless it rang each day he never noticed time—but this day he merely said, 'Turn that off, Ed Baird.' We were still at it at 4 P.M.," according to the memory of senior Horace Poynter, who made a career of teaching the classics at Phillips Andover.

At last, Old Johnny stopped his brilliant inquisition. He sat silent for a moment or two. He gazed at the proud, steady faces before him. His eyes grew wet with tears of joy. He took out his handkerchief and blew his nose rather vigorously. As the winter shadows grew longer, he finally spoke: "That is the most beautiful gift I have ever received. We shall begin the *Iliad* tomorrow."

Yet Old Johnny brought far more than tears and gentleness to his teaching repertoire. Very rarely, he became stern. Occasionally, he used his critical sharp mind for a pointed irony. To a boy who avoided answering in Greek class on grounds he was a stammerer, but who managed to give public declamations on Friday afternoon, Old Johnny said: "There seems to be a slight periodicity about your stammering." He gave one boy a nickname by exposing his white lie. The boy insisted he was paying attention and that he also understood an obscure point Old Johnny was making. He caught the boy empty-eared and empty-headed. "I was waiting for that to percolate," said the teacher, and the irony turned the boy into "Percolator," or "Perks," for life.

One morning in pleasant weather, when some minds find it so hard to work, he told a sleepy girl, "Miss Jennie, perhaps you'll wake yourself up if you'll walk down to the curved bridge and back. . . ." She did not like it much, but she huffed and puffed the half mile south toward Wartrace to the spot where the railroad passes the swimming hole, and made her return. On an especially slow morning, Old Johnny had all the boys run the several miles northward to Fosterville and back simply to wake them up. Of a mid-morning, if he found a class did not seem to know their lessons,

he would close his eyes, shake his head, and send them back outdoors. They knew, without being told, not to re-enter the Senior
Room until they knew their work. Sometimes, he went to midday
"dinner" and left the seniors on their class grounds, where they remained. He was never known to utter a cross word.

He knew how to acknowledge a mistake. A group of boys were
taking an examination on Hall and Knight's university algebra, a
particularly difficult text for seniors then. They had eight problems
to solve. They worked all morning and were still at work, no one
finished, when Old Johnny came in at two. Johnny looked at Clovis
Chappell's paper, returned it to its owner, and said, "I have made
the examination too hard. Anybody who gets six will have a perfect
paper."

There were mornings when Johnny sat in his room reading a
book. As students entered on schedule, one after another, Johnny
kept reading, moving his lips. He always read aloud to himself.
When he became conscious of the students around him, he raised
his musical voice, and continued reading, sometimes until a student had to remind him, "Mr. Webb, it's 12 o'clock."

He followed no rigid timetable, and set no order of classroom
subjects. Especially on a book like the *Iliad*, the boys might spend
a month without touching another text. The learning was so thorough that seniors often translated an accurate English version back
into the Greek. He was overjoyed when he received from Cam-
bridge University Press one of the first school editions of a Shake-
spearean play. He took the opportunity of bringing more works of
English literature into the curriculum.

He employed the stratagem of pulling off a library shelf some
book he especially admired, or found timely and appropriate, and
laying it where a senior would be certain to pick it up. He noticed
a very bright senior had read *King Lear* on his own, and he proceeded to follow quotation after quotation with searching questions. His conclusion: "Probably you should read it again, more
carefully." The youth said he read it three times before Old Johnny
could be persuaded that he had absorbed from it all that he could
be expected to gain from such a tragedy.

The library was John Webb's kingdom. The selection of books
had been his exclusive responsibility since his arrival at Culleoka
in 1873. His disciple John Andrew Rice gives this perceptive picture: ". . . The books were not adolescent nor for adolescents; for

he knew the young want to grow. He chose mainly what he liked to read himself, and they were put on the shelves in some spiritual order that would make a student of 'library science' shudder. The *Origin of Species* might sit between the poems of Keats and Lane's *Latin Grammar* and be none the worse for the company. He was no Aristotelian; he knew the limits and poison of classification."

He was a man of many thousand books. As his son Albert majored in French at Yale, he followed the curriculum himself, studying both language and phonetics from the best textbooks and commentaries. His French pronunciation was reported to be nearly perfect. In one year alone he read some eighty books in French—almost all the novels of Balzac and René Bazin, and became amazingly well informed about the currents of French theology. This Methodist-reared teacher even chose to read President Domergue's monumental life of the supreme predestinarian, John Calvin. "You must go to sources to find what man really thought and believed; you cannot take the labels of men," he said.

When his academic "son" Edwin Mims decided to do graduate work in English, John Webb surprised him by often being able to guide his study better than some of Mims's university professors. "Many were the talks that we had on Wordsworth, Tennyson, and Browning at a time when I was just discovering them," Mims recalled.

His home on the west side of Maple Street was a two-story under-statement of Victorian tracery, buff-colored with dark green shutters. The capitals of the porch pillars appeared to be fleur-de-lis in a daylight blend of light and shadow. The front porch stopped short on the left, where the library began. By the turn of the century the ubiquitous shelves were double-stacked to the ceiling. Books overflowed into every room and eventually into the attic.

A new student from a backwoods area came from a family who had been proud to own "*a* book." When he first visited Sawney's he was surprised by the roomful of books there. Later, he was astounded on a visit to John Webb's home at the scholar's far larger and more varied collection. Finally, he was stupefied one evening at Sawney Webb's, when Brother John arrived, and asked: "Sawney, have you anything to read?"

John started a Dante Club for his own children, nieces and nephews, which later grew to include other villagers. One of Sawney's daughters said: "Many a time have I held his gentle hand as he climbed the golden stairway, watching for the heavenly flash-lights of Beatrice. . . . I vividly recall how fascinated I was with the varied and dramatic sufferings which were visited upon the exiles of eternity . . . when on the other hand, I was always chilled to the bone with terror, whenever my father happened to read in family prayers, the Gospel description of the place where the 'worm dieth not and the fire is not quenched.' "

He took his love of Dante to nearby towns, and on to Nashville, where he gave weekly lectures and readings to the Centennial Club. From the days of his courtship, he enjoyed friendships among the best minds of the Vanderbilt faculty. He met with their Greek Club. He was a charter member and onetime president of the state Philological Society. He was always gladly learning and gladly teaching at all kinds of academic and religious gatherings. He remained too human to succumb to a narrow specialism.

He heard a southern preacher deliver a tirade against both lynching and "higher criticism." He heartily concurred in the attack on lynching. No one was more deeply disturbed by that regional disgrace than he. But he asked the preacher afterward what higher criticism was. When the minister replied that he did not know, John Webb remarked, "Well, brother, you lynched higher criticism today."

He quietly tried to influence the intellectual advance against provincialism and religious bigotry. He did not believe that the free life of the mind need wreck the faith of a man, and former students reported that thanks to him, the critical approach to the Bible never shook their foundations of belief, as it did for so many of their friends. He sharply criticized the policy of a leading southern Methodist bishop at the publishing house: "H—— keeps a double stock in non-communicating departments—one brand for foreign consumption and one strictly for the home market. The foreign brand is 'pure food' but the home brand is adulterated." John Webb unintentionally caused a new pastor to startle his Bell Buckle congregation one Sunday morning. The pastor announced that in case of sickness or distress in the home of members he would gladly come, on call. Otherwise he had too much work to do in his study. Blame the scholar's wisdom and books for overwhelming his young friend.

In 1895 the University of Nashville, later renamed George Peabody College for Teachers, awarded John an honorary doctorate.

The same year, the Southern Association of Colleges and Schools was founded for the express purpose of improving education throughout the South. At first only a small membership could qualify. It started with seven colleges. Two other institutions, one of them Webb at Bell Buckle, had the honor of becoming secondary-school charter members.

From the beginning John Webb was a member of the SACS executive committee. In 1899 this unaggressive man became president of the association. He spoke little, but he did submit, by request, a list of 278 volumes, to cost little more than $300, as a nucleus for a suitable secondary-school library. "I have had before me," he said, "the needs of Southern schools, especially in rural districts, where there is a dearth of libraries, public and private. The problem is to put into the hands of the susceptible, but untrained, youth a book that will awaken and direct a latent literary taste, hasten the emotions, and form character, leading at last to a taste for the world's best literature." The list enjoyed a wide distribution.

The several years on both sides of the turn of the century were very likely the happiest of his lifetime. Certainly they were most fulfilling. His quiet role in the advancement of learning was never clearer. Erudite men in the East as well as the South gave him chief credit for the remarkably superior college preparation of Webb graduates.

Bell Buckle merchants found him surprisingly practical. He was actually elected president of the Bell Buckle Bank because of his sound business sense. Many acquaintances came to him for advice about investments. He seemed to have a photographic memory for significant details. He built up a tidy portfolio of securities for a schoolmaster, although he spent relatively little time on them.

He cultivated his garden. He enjoyed long walks. He took part in the bicycle fad of the nineties with great enthusiasm, threatening to cycle all the way to North Carolina if the roads were good.

With quiet joy, he watched his three lovely daughters grow up, and he was grateful for their devotion to him. The elite of southern academic circles enjoyed the hospitality of his home. His wife Lily was the completely equipped hostess for such gatherings. She was cultivated in the conversation of ideas, her parlor reflected a quiet elegance of good taste in mahogany and oriental rugs, and her table was consistent with her motto that "fried chicken should be so greaseless that one could eat it wearing white kid gloves." Lily was, for all her daintiness, a strong personality with a talent for home management, intense in her convictions. Like her husband, she was lonely in the rural village.

John's affinity to children created a wide circle of young admirers. Some of them followed him into his library where he read to them. The son of a Methodist minister, after leaving Bell Buckle at the age of three years and ten months, was able to recite the first one hundred lines of *Lady of the Lake* without missing a line, and with occasional correction went through one hundred fifty lines, often substituting a word which proved he had grasped the meaning. He had learned from listening to his friend John Webb. Whenever the scholar traveled—even once when he was being rushed east for surgery—he sent picture postcards to his small friends.

During his son Albert's stint at Yale, John met one of the university's distinguished professors, C. C. Clarke, at a summer resort in Rhode Island. John's breadth of knowledge astounded the professor. He would interrupt John's conversation with, "Now wait, and let me write down the name of that author and that book." He remarked to Albert afterward: "I did not know that there were any men left in the world like Mr. Webb. He has had time to learn so much in such a broad way and of so many things. We university specialists cannot do that."

Certain developments in education deeply troubled John M. Webb. He was disturbed by an effort in North Carolina to oust a liberal-minded professor named John Spencer Bassett from Trinity College, which later became Duke University. "Trinity," he wrote his close friend Professor Edwin Mims, "is the only unmistakably unprovincial, yet pos [i] tively ethical college we have. Should she let Bassett go she drops into line with Emory and localizes herself. I say only; for while Vanderbilt is broad enough there is not an ethical spirit manifesting itself organically, however noble some of the members are." He deplored the attacks on Bassett by "persons who have never patronized Trinity." He sought a "middle way" between a liberal and secular institution of higher education, and the "ethical" but narrow type of religious college.

But John Webb was most disturbed by the zeal of management-minded educators to improve the schools by basing them on mechanical principles—schools were looking suspiciously like industrial plants already. "I wish I were 'pope' long enough to put 'standardization' on the index," he wrote Mims as early as 1908.

The ubiquitous Carnegie Unit, which bases academic credit on the number of hours a student spends in the classroom, was just being strongly advanced as the supreme answer to improving the quality of national education. "When you push by external pressure a fourteen-unit standard into the catalog, how are you going to preserve the quality of the unit? Ten honest units is better than fourteen dubious ones," John wrote in a letter.

The Southern Association of Colleges and Schools was behind the movement. So was Chancellor Kirkland of Vanderbilt, guiding spirit of the association. The university was putting pressure on its tributary schools to conform. Students who could present certification of Carnegie Units were being admitted without examination. These developments sent fifteen of the best secondary-school educators of the state into closed conference in March of 1911. John reported to Mims that "they all agreed that the morale of the student body [at Vanderbilt] was worse than it ever has been in the history of the institution." Most of the participants were strong supporters of Kirkland on other issues.

"Control," he wrote, "seems to be the dominating motive. I cannot make the fourteen units honestly enforced with [out] surrendering quality to quantity. To do so would be to go back on history & say that forty years' work for the real & genuine was a mistake. Whither shall I flee from this tyranny?" Once he confessed to Mims, "Perhaps I ought not to write so freely, but I am so isolated here that I must have a safety valve & you will not get me into trouble." Old Johnny became known as Old Jack among students during these years. He continued his inspirational teaching. "I do not think my classroom work was ever better than it is now," he confided to Mims. "But to feel so may be a sign that the sun is westering."

His greatest anguish was a development within his family—and it went to the heart of the school itself. It was enough to tear his gentle spirit in two.

Strong-minded Lily and strong-minded Sawney clashed. Encounters led to vehement disagreements. The brother knew he was not welcome in Lily's house and stopped visiting. Sawney's children remembered John's sorrowfully crossing the street more than once to apologize to his older brother for something Lily had said. John's own children had reacted with antipathy to Sawney's aggressive style in the classroom. Their uncle was so unlike their mild-mannered father. It was easy to believe he was being hard on them, especially when Sawney told Albert that as a member of the family he had better behave because punishments would come in double doses if he did not.

Sawney's position widened the rift. The circular always listed both brothers as "Principals," but it was obvious that Sawney actually ran the school. Then on the return of Son Will, and his appointment as a principal in 1908, it seemed to the John Webb family that Sawney was seeking a monopoly. Hopes had almost crystallized into an assumption that John's son Albert would join Sawney's son in the school partnership. Sawney, however, could neither agree with Albert's opinions about changing school policy, nor appreciate his nephew's gratuitous remarks. Resentments deepened and bitterness grew. John must have suffered the most in the spiritual war between his dearest ones and the brother whom he had so many reasons to love.

It was more than "enough to make the angels weep." Yet villagers were hardly aware of the family trouble. It did not come to a dramatic head until the year of John Webb's death.

XIV. A Most Improbable Road to Washington

*I never met a man
in my life
without learning
something from him.*
—SAWNEY WEBB

The boy who particularly touched the heart of Old Sawney was the shy one, the poor one, the ignorant one, the one who felt inferior, unsure, underprivileged, or afraid, yet was in deep earnest under his desperation. "Don't talk to me about blue-bloods that sit at the foot of the class," he would say. "If that's so, I'd rather have soapsuds or frogspawn in my veins. . . . I'm for the scrub horse that's got the 'go' in him."

Old Sawney fashioned the true history of a little scrub horse into a fable about the human spirit. He was certain he himself had once muffed a chance to buy him. In the cavernous Big Room, boys twelve to twenty heard it. In "Lousy Levels" all over the South, they heard it. A scrub is a "poor insignificant person" as well as a "domestic animal of inferior breed." Sawney aimed his story at the "poor insignificant person," and he told it something like this:

Years ago when I lived in Culleoka, I went to the county fair. A colored man came up to me and said, "Mr. Webb, won't you buy this little horse from me?" He was a trim little horse.

"Is he a blood horse?" I asked.

"Naw sir, no blooded horse, but he sure has got the 'go' in him."

"How much do you want for him?"

"Seventy-five dollars."

"I don't want any scrub," I replied, "I want a thoroughbred."

I paid $100 for the horse I bought that day. A neighbor bought the scrub, strapped him to an old two-wheeled surrey, and drove away from the Fairgrounds. Just then a man driving a beautiful bay hitched to a new buggy came thundering up behind and started to pass the scrub.

"What's this you're going to do?" the little horse said. "Pass me? Well, not much!"

It was not long before he was tossing dust back into the face of that big horse. He was a scrub, but he seemed to say: "Come on with that shiny buggy, and pass me if you can."

The new owner said, "Well, he surely has got the 'go' in him, but he's a scrub. He never will hold that gait." But he did, and the new owner got to thinking: "I believe I'll give him a blooded horse's chance."

The owner fed him carefully, rubbed him down, and exercised him, then entered him in his first harness race. He lined up with the other horses, the old starter waved his handkerchief, and the scrub found himself on the outside, the hardest place to run.

But he didn't whine or cry. He didn't say, "They ought not to put me in the class with these town boys—I've never had a chance." He said, "All my life I've heard that blueblood is for running purposes. I'll just see what's in it."

He tore around the track. He nosed over and got away from the outside. He passed one horse: "Well, I trapped one of them," he said. He passed another and another. He took the lead on the inside. The scrub horse came streaking under the wire, a winner.

My son, here's some actual history. I've been told that horse in six months sold for $1400, and within a short time sold for much, much more. He became one of the most famous horses in the history of harness racing: Little Brown Jug!

One day, leaning out of my schoolhouse window at Culleoka, I saw Major Campbell Brown with the strangest-looking drove of horses you can imagine. I went out and said, "Major, what are you going to do with all those horses?"

"Sawney," he replied, "you see that old horse over there? That is Tom Hal, and he's the sire of Little Brown Jug. I just bought him and all of Little Brown Jug's kinfolks I could find."

Now, one of the finest lines of harness-racing stock in the country goes back to Tom Hal, sire of Little Brown Jug, the little scrub horse with the "go" in him.

My son, I want you to do what Little Brown Jug did. I want you to go out into the world and pedigree your ancestors!

A Negro farmer really did buy Little Brown Jug for $75, and he did have to sell the horse in the mid-1870s, about the time Sawney bought another. The purchaser did discover the horse's uncommonly fast pacing gait. By 1878, the Jug actually was appearing in harness races. In 1879 he was being trained at Lewisburg over the county line from Culleoka. Two years later he was racing up North on the Grand Circuit. On August 24, 1884, at Hartford, Little Brown Jug did set the world's pacing record for the mile at 2:11¾.

Buyers did go "scurrying" to Tennessee for other horses of his kind, and Major Brown bought up all the Hals he could find, and gave Mr. Harness Racing himself, Ed Geers, the challenge of training the Hal line. It is even true that the Jug was a factor in establishing a harness-racing pedigree, the so-called "Standard Bred" criterion, in the late nineteenth century, and that he also helped to make the pacing gait respectable. "No gentleman drives a pacer," had been a dictum of horse fanciers for many years before.

Pedigree your ancestors. Give your granddaddies a proud name. Have not Americans of all races from every inhabited part of the earth been doing just that since this nation first became a new idea?

"My son, listen to me, I want to repeat," Sawney declared, "there isn't a boy here, never has been, that can't do well in life if he will try. But somebody comes along and says: 'I want to be pre-eminent.' You have no right to expect it. . . . My son, I am going to try to rise above the average by hard work, but if I can just get up to a good average, I will be mighty comfortable. . . . If you can't do big things, just do your best."

Old Sawney himself had renounced the "big things" long ago. A war had blown up his dream of statesmanship. He would try to live the largest life he could—in a very small place. Home was headquarters. It stood far back in a shady yard on the east side of Maple Street, across from the smaller residence of his brother. Matched pairs of Ionic pillars stood guard on the sprawling front porch. The two-story Roman mass arose behind it. Several brick chimneys towered above the red-roofed gables to give breath to the grate fires on colder days. The attic served two rising generations as a skating rink when it rained. The noise of active children was happy music.

"Sawney House" was destined to become a boys' dormitory. A special side entrance brought boys to his book-lined office. The door was open at any time of the day or evening. He left his door literally open, even in winter, and sat in his spindle-backed rocker, reading the daily newspaper and the *Congressional Record*. On his rolltop desk lay jumbled piles of papers, letters, and only-Sawney-knew-what. Note-sized slips and papers filled most of the pigeon holes. Here he sorted out checks and made entries in a ponderous old ledger—tuition payments, bills for assorted purposes, boys' allowances. "I have spent my life buying galluses and shoestrings for boys," he sometimes complained. But he taught them never to waste their money.

In this seldom-dusted vicinity he endured the war-throb in his shoulder, and forced his disabled hand to do his will. For decades he wrote in a barely legible scrawl an endless number of letters—reports to parents, job recommendations for old boys, support for a variety of public causes, invitations to guest speakers. He also handled farm business and other investments here. He would borrow money to buy acreages of promise. Cautious land speculation kept him independent. He had an uncanny key to the apparent chaos on his desk. He went to one of many jumbled piles, grabbed the tip of one paper, and shook loose whatever he wanted. Once a well-meaning servant, in the absence of wife Emma who would have stopped her, decided it was her job to straighten up his desk. On his return from the schoolhouse, he was incensed at the spurious order. The poor servant ran out of the house and never came back. When Son Will was about to be married to Louise Hall Manning, Sawney told him, "You have a chance now and it's the last chance you'll ever have—you must get an agreement that she'll *never* clean up your desk."

In Bell Buckle he once again suffered adversity. "My bank broke me in 1893," he recalled. It was a panic year, but he always believed crooked management had caused his old bank in Columbia to fail. As a director, he was deeply involved. "It did not impair my credit to break, as I met everything," he told his lawyer son Clary, "though it took all my resources to do so. . . . I made good nearly $3,000 belonging to patrons of the school though under no obligations to do so. It paid me in the end. . . ."

In 1896 he took a stand that, his friends warned, would cause him to lose patrons for certain. He campaigned for the Gold Standard all over the state. It made him very unpopular and subjected him to public attack. Brother John called Sawney's efforts "pure patriotism."

A brilliant young Memphis editor debated with him vigorously. It was his red-headed, dimple-faced student Ned Carmack. The old boy wore a handsome auburn brush mustache. He had grown into a powerful man. Sawney could not seem to avoid repeated confrontations with this one-time rebel against his discipline. Yet he emphatically believed that, sound money or not, Ned was destined to do the big things.

"Professor" Webb was a Tennessee delegate that year to the Goldbug Convention that nominated Palmer and Buckner. He was the grandson of a congressman known in his family as "the Daddy of the Dollar"—he was an old student of a teacher who accepted only hard money as tuition. He could never support a standard-breaking man like Bryan. His "sound money" stand was the beginning of his strange career as a public figure. He used it to wage war on southern ignorance.

He told his student body with emphatic exaggeration, "We have got the smallest number of educated men on the face of the earth."

"Mr. Webb, you are not loyal to the South."

"I spilled my blood for the South. . . . What's the use in trying to deny the facts?"

He helped former students to start new schools and overcome state and regional illiteracy. Clovis Chappell organized a lecture series to raise money for a public library, and he invited Sawney to be first on the program. Only about one hundred townspeople showed up in the thousand-seat opera house. Sawney noticed the depressed look on his old boy's face after the lecture. "Son, if everybody were as interested in public libraries as they ought to be, the Lord wouldn't need you and me," Sawney told him. "But they're not and that is the reason He put us here."

At the 1902 General Conference, he fought off floor opposition to a recommendation that all young Methodist ministers undergo theological training. As the drive for good public education gained momentum, he went everywhere he could to encourage the establishment of high schools. Sawney Webb refused to join other private educators who fought free schools because they feared them. In a widely circulated speech, he declared they were "in no sense rivals." The public and private high schools "are to each other supplementary."

In 1904, he declined the presidency of the University of Tennessee, communicating his decision through his cousin and old-time Bingham schoolmate, who now was a resident of Knoxville. Shap Webb wrote back, "I think you have acted wisely. The Board of Trustees have sometimes greatly hampered the President & faculty, and, if you had accepted, I was intending to advise you to stipulate a free hand."

So the old educational independent continued to travel the dusty country roads in his rough-riding buckboard, bent down on one side where he so often sat and mused alone. In later years he hitched this "stripped-down" buggy to a good steady horse he named Ned Carmack. "Not fast quarter-horse racing but steady four-mile gait," he often said. He would stop at a little roadside church, enter the empty vestibule, and place some books he thought might fire the imagination of some boy or girl. With his own funds he equipped twenty-two traveling libraries. Later the state itself took over his private program.

Sawney felt the hill people especially needed him. On speaking trips he often met impressive young men. He always invited them to come and study with him. It is impossible to estimate the number of tuition scholarships that Sawney and John made possible through the years. If he had to choose between addressing prominent city people and talking to hill people far out on difficult roads, he invariably accepted the farmers' invitation.

He talked the plain talk of country people (in common with Mississippi's later Nobel Prize winner in literature). He even said he would rather have a boy say "I seen it" when he really saw something than to say "I saw it" and not see anything. He was a master of large crowds. Before and after his many speeches, he could go into his Confederate crouch and talk weather, politics, or crops.

But he reserved his combative passions for Prohibition. He thought he knew its value from his struggle at Culleoka. Prohibition was a vanguard of civilization, an enemy to violence, a brace for the forward march toward self-control. Such a law could "check the appetites of the weaker natures." Such a law could save them from self-enslavement. What if newspapers at first refused to report the drys' activities? What if others scoffed at their "Sunday School politics" and called them cranks?

Sunday School politics led Sawney to lobby with state legislators. He became a favorite with the Anti-Saloon League. He praised the Women's Christian Temperance Union. The dry cause began winning widespread support. Sawney stumped for Prohibition all over the nation, and he said he was paid nothing more than a pocket knife for his efforts. Not every "temperance lecturer" could say the same.

Then his "old boy" Ned Carmack switched to the "right side" of the question. At this change of mind, Old Sawney was overjoyed. He had gone to hear Ned open his first campaign for the senate. He sat with the candidate on the train during their return. All the younger man could talk about was his little son, and Sawney listened with great interest. Finally the old teacher said earnestly, "Ned, that son of yours is robbed of his birthright by his own father." Ned resented the remark with spirit and demanded an explanation. Sawney said that the father had robbed his son of a Christian training. Ned replied that the mother would attend to that.

Several years afterwards, as Sawney entered another train, Ned, now a United States senator, called him over and told him the boy should have his birthright: Carmack had finally joined a Christian church. Sawney was also deeply gratified when he heard Carmack's speech on "character." It was in far more fancy language than the old teacher tried to use, but it was filled with echoes of Sawney's own lectures. He proudly watched Ned perform on the national scene as keynote speaker at the Democratic convention, as featured orator at Richmond on the unveiling of a statue of Robert E. Lee. Ned was recognized as one of the ablest leaders of his party. He looked forward to a brilliant future. He had a tall, erect figure, an old-time orator's abundant hair, the appearance of an auburn-haired Mark Twain. He retained the warm winsomeness of his boyhood, and his wide range of wit and humor was becoming famous.

However, another witty orator named Robert Taylor defeated him for re-election to the Senate, and Carmack's friends blamed liquor interests for the setback. The ex-senator returned to journalism. He became editor of the pro-temperance *Nashville Tennessean*. He attacked his political enemies in a clever style that could be so bitingly satirical as to infuriate them. Carmack carried a pistol in public. He particularly delighted in deriding Major Duncan Brown Cooper, as "the little bald-headed angel from hell." Carmack so often angered Cooper that he was reported giving warning that Carmack had better not mention his name in print again. On November 9, 1908, Carmack called him something new: "The diplomat of the political Zweibund," a man "who made soda and vinegar to dwell placidly in the same bottle," with several other printed lines of nonsensical-sounding innuendo. That afternoon, pistol shots rang out in downtown Nashville and Carmack fell on the cobblestones, fatally shot in the neck.

"Carmack Assassinated!" the headlines screamed on November 10. In jail were Major Cooper and his son Robin. A bullet from Robin's gun was the cause of death. The *Tennessean* produced pictures of the pair on page one, and labeled the portly, walrus-mustached Cooper "the mouthpiece of the liquor interests." Who fired the first shot was in dispute from the beginning. A woman who was chatting with Carmack at the time said Robin fired first. The Coopers claimed Carmack grabbed for his pistol and fired, just as the Major raised his finger merely to signal he wanted to talk. The Coopers were later convicted, but the father was pardoned and the son finally freed of all charges after the state supreme court had ordered a new trial for him. The question remains as controversial as politics and family dignity.

The state was in turmoil. Neighbors quarreled and fought. Kinfolks of the Coopers were battered defending their honor. An enraged crowd of Carmack's Columbia friends and supporters took the evening train to Nashville to break into the jail. When Mrs. Carmack heard they were coming, she sent a close friend of the family to meet them. At her request they returned home without any violence. The nation was stirred. Indignant editorials appeared in newspapers across the country. "No savage land has more murders than parts of America," cried the *Rochester* (N.Y.) *Post Express.*

This public death of his dearest old boy shook Sawney with a riot of emotions. The bullet that struck down Carmack ruptured a ganglion of the old teacher's cherished hopes and convictions. On his own sixty-sixth birthday, he attended the funeral in Columbia, and served as an honorary pallbearer. He watched as the body of the younger man was laid to rest. Old Sawney did not doubt that Ned was "the greatest man our state has produced . . . his lifeblood was too precious . . . to stain the cobblestones of Nashville."

". . . And if I had had the genius and courage of Senator Carmack, my blood too would have been poured upon the street long ago," he wrote his youngest daughter. "Whiskey will make a man kill his child, his wife, his parents, himself. Murder and assassination always accompany this accursed traffic." Yet he was certain it was "whiskey's expiring blow." The political reaction did legally dry up Tennessee.

On Sunday, November 15, thousands of indignant Tennesseans thronged the slopes of downtown Nashville around Fifth Avenue, near a red-brick Cathedral to Temperance, destined to become the Capitol of Country Music. They walked beneath the tiers of white-trimmed arched windows and flocked through the wide front doors. They jammed the spacious hall that a onetime whiskey dealer had erected in honor of the famous revivalist Sam Jones, who had reformed him. They filled the curved pews and overflowed into the new Confederate gallery. Palms and giant vases of white chrysanthemums decorated the stage of Ryman Auditorium, and all dignitaries seated on the platform wore red carnations.

On a two-hour program of eulogies and hymns, Sawney talked for less than twenty minutes. His voice remained close to breaking and he fought back bitterness and tears: "E. W. Carmack was a genius and only another genius can penetrate his words and actions to the spirit beneath them . . . I have no such capacity . . . I knew him as a rollicking, fun-loving boy . . . Senator Carmack was an honest man—not one pre-election promise unfulfilled in all his history. Faultless? No. As an honest man, he would not have me say so here today . . . Senator Carmack was a great man . . . Carmack was no meteor. He was a great and steady light."

Faultless? No. The very trait that resulted in Ned's final departure from Webb School decades before had brought him to a death in his own blood. It was his penchant for invective, his relentless ridicule of those who inspired his annoyance and dislike. Old Sawney in the depths of his grieving heart must have known it. He dwelt, however, on the evil done. "The hardest thing I ever tried to do was talk about Ned and not say bitter things," he wrote a friend. "I found it necessary to write and read every word. . . . I am still human."

He did not feel well on his return to Bell Buckle, but he continued to give his Big Room lectures. Thanksgiving Day was his last appearance in 1908, and his final word was the instruction that a little boy who had neglected writing home should come up on Saturday and spend the morning composing a letter to his mother.

Before the year ended, he went west on Mr. Harriman's transcontinental railroad. After Thanksgiving, he had taken to his bed and grown dangerously ill. Pneumonia then was deadly to a physically spent and emotionally exhausted old man. Sawney thought he was going west to die. His son John met him in California. John took him to the dry Coachella Valley, and showed him how "they pull out the stopper" of irrigation when they need rain, and make the desert bloom. Old Sawney settled down and felt a little vigor returning. The dry heat penetrated his body and baked his lungs. Before long he was out working like a farmer on the rich land, hardly realizing it could be the dead of winter. The old boyish spirit revived. He visited, and went sightseeing in Los Angeles. He saw grapevines that did not bear fruit being thrown into piles and burned, just like those that Jesus talked about, and he tucked the scene away for some future "Gospel of Do" chapel talk to his boys. "This is the most valuable piece of the earth," he wrote back home with enthusiasm, and decided to buy some acreage at bargain prices. He arrived back in Bell Buckle in the spring of 1909 like a man returned from the edge of the grave.

In his absence, Son Will had started running the school. Upon hearing of the drive to eradicate hookworm in the South, Will wrote the Rockefeller Sanitary Commission to send a team to Bell Buckle and Bedford County. The descriptive term "lazy man's disease" enraged supersensitive southerners. But a southern educator, Dr. Wickliffe Rose from Nashville, fortunately brought wise and successful leadership to the program, and later took his hookworm teams around the earth. The significance was not lost on the intense old man. He remembered the dull-eyed boys that simply would not learn and he remembered his attempts to "agitate their nervous systems." "We didn't know it, son, but we've been cruel monsters in our day," he said passionately. "No boy ought ever to be whipped until the doctors have checked him over and say there's nothing to keep the boy from learning."

Public health also demanded changes in "Egypt," the secluded campus privy. Wooden boards with holes and an open drain below gave way to metal seats over a ditch that had no outlet. The accumulations of human waste could be safely burned under cover of metal, nightfall, and the trees that hid the place from view. Old Sawney was proud of the school's New Egypt.

Progress made him an optimist. The establishment of the World

Court at The Hague caused him to remember with some pride his
own ill-fated public speech at Horner's. He called the Court "the
greatest step toward peace since Christ's coming." Technological
progress, like the coming of the horseless carriage, also excited him,
though he still preferred "a man" to any thing, and he never let his
boys forget it: "My son, I'd rather have a job as U.S. Senator and
talents like Ned Carmack had than sit back in wealthy obscurity
and ride in an auto and wear fur coats," he said.

Of course, his use of "I" was a subtle *alter ego* for "my son." It
was a constant technique of his fatherhood. He could never have
consciously thought of what he was literally saying. Yet he sat one
night in 1912 on a bench in a Memphis railroad station, and confessed to an "old boy" that he did not feel his fellow Tennesseans
had shown him full appreciation for his efforts on behalf of education, that he knew he was close to the end of his career. A few
months later, the telephone rang long distance for W. R. Webb in
Bell Buckle. It was a call from the state capital. He could not believe the news, which would be on the front pages of every Tennessee daily the next morning: Old Sawney was United States senator-
elect. The legislature after a long deadlock had chosen him by a
decisive vote.

The village schoolmaster was going to Washington to sit in the
chamber of what he himself had called in his eulogy to Carmack
"the most august body of men on earth." This old Latin teacher
with a Roman nose, who read the latest *Congressional Record* along
with his daily newspaper, who kept a miniature portrait of his congressman grandfather on the mantel in his front parlor, would serve
in the very senatorial seat that had belonged to his dearest "old
boy."

XV. The Sunlight, and the Shadow, of Publicity

The highest type of man
that has ever been on this earth,
"when he was reviled,
reviled not again."
—SAWNEY WEBB

"*I'll show you how Old Sawney's going to do* when he gets in the Senate." An excited little boy was prancing across the platform of the Big Room, aping the new United States senator from Bell Buckle, and preparing his throat for a soprano imitation of the old man's tenor twang: "He's going to get up in that room some day and say: 'Senators, this bill has got to pass, and that quick. I hope it can be done pleasantly.' "

It was early 1913. Virtually everything from the village to Nashville, to Washington, and back was done pleasantly. The vigorous old man prepared his acceptance speech as he marched up Tennessee's Capitol Hill on January 27. He scrawled eighteen words, even less legible than usual, on three sheets of a small note pad. The eighteenth word was *Carmack*.

He entered the towering Temple of Law, hewn and carved out of native limestone to neoclassical ideals, and flanked with the familiar Ionic columns. Inside, the state legislature awaited him in joint session. A tri-partisan coalition had elected him to the unexpired term of the late Senator Robert Taylor. The new white-bearded junior senator appeared before the lawmakers almost overcome with emotion, spectacles on his nose, and the three scraps of paper in his hand. He thanked all his audience, for they had made their final vote for him unanimous. He acknowledged that his "senatorial toga" was only seven weeks short. He admitted his record in politics was "an absolute blank." He also reminded them where he stood. "The paramount issue of state politics of late years began with me when I was quite a little kid and my widowed mother, within sight of the smoke of distilleries, took me on her knee and told me it was wrong to make whiskey and wrong to sell it to men."

He reviewed his strenuous life. He described the anarchy he had lived with. "I have never had a hand in the making of a law, but I know how to obey laws," he said. As he looked out among these men who did make laws, he saw a number of his "old boys." "I never dreamed of this honor," he said. "I was talking to my wife, telling her of the utter impossibility of my election, when the telephone rang . . . I—I was to fill Senator Carmack's seat. He was a great genius and a great statesman, and I wish today he was in that seat himself."

On the night before he took the train to Washington, he was guest of honor at a banquet given by a large number of the Webb old boys—business and professional men, farmers, educators. As their spokesman, attorney Walter Stokes declared: "Here is the man who has done more for the South than any other man who has ever lived in it. . . . A man of matchless genius, and unflinching courage."

Sawney never thought of himself as a genius, but he was grateful: "God knows that it gives me the greatest possible pleasure to see my boys, who have developed into fine men. It is a matter of amazement to me that God has spared me so long. I have often been in places of danger. And now the state has taken me by surprise. . . . When they told me that I was going to be elected, it seemed like a joke. It still seems like a dream. I attribute it all to the partiality and kindness of my students."

They had, in fact, chosen to elect that irascible old man who had harassed them through their difficult years into manhood. Did they sense that this was both the resurrection and fulfillment of a Whig Unionist's boyish dream of long ago? It certainly was one Big Cosmic Joke on a 70-year-old village schoolmaster.

The morning after his arrival in Washington, he found empty whiskey bottles outside his room. He changed hotels immediately. The veteran of a village whiskey war was sure that some of his foes would stop at nothing to discredit him. He also knew he whetted the desire of some people to find evidence he was an arrant hypocrite. His wife and two daughters, Alla and Emma, were with him. They were more than companionship, they were Victorian protection. They had successfully prevailed on him to acquire a new wardrobe: a Prince Albert coat, a new black Stetson hat, even a new black string tie—as well as a new overcoat which was much against his will.

On February 3 he took the oath of office in his new clothes at the Capitol. He attended a banquet of North Carolinians and paid tribute to his native state as the "mother" of his dear Tennessee. He coped with hundreds of office seekers and cranks, including a man who insisted that he introduce federal legislation to bar all "bad boys" from school. He gave a eulogy to the Tennessee senator who had died in office. He took a wreath to the old Congressional Cemetery and laid it on the grave of his maternal grandfather, Congressman Richard Stanford, who had also died in office.

He coaxed the solemn face of Senator Henry Cabot Lodge into a half-hour smile by praising the dour New Englander's book about his boyhood. The incident so piqued the curiosity of newsmen that the dean of the press gallery pursued Senator Webb to his office to find out what he could possibly have said to Lodge. The press made good news copy of the eccentric old Confederate veteran. New York newspapers reported his story of escape from Battery Prison. Books and magazines began garbling the story, and since then he has been reported as having escaped from several other islands, and as having swum hundreds of yards (with his throbbing shoulder) to the shore of Manhattan. One newspaper even reported he was log-cabin born. Such a character simply had to be.

When Senator Webb arose to make his major speech, the gallery was packed. Conversation was also buzzing loudly all over the Senate chamber. His daughter Alla, in the gallery opposite, was to signal him if she could not hear. He would not address an inattentive audience. He waited. Only when the house was quiet did he start his speech.

He drew upon classical mythology to prove that strong drink was an ancient evil. He paid tribute to Senator Carmack as a "martyr" to the temperance cause. He declared, "The world is getting better"—a faith he kept. He offered as evidence his own lifetime experiences of disorder and violence now overcome: "Duelling was common. A gentleman allowed himself to be punctured into a pepper box to show that he was brave." The field of dishonor was indeed a vice of the past. "I saw in my boyhood liquor absolutely without restriction. It is now restricted in a thousand ways."

He spoke in favor of a new restriction: a bill to prohibit interstate shipment of beverage alcohol into all-dry states, which now included Tennessee. He was overwhelmed as the audience applauded. "I came near fainting. . . . A page set a glass of water on the desk, and a film-guard over my eye, and I just did have enough sense to get that water." The bill he favored passed both Senate and House, but lame-duck President Taft vetoed the measure. Later Sawney joined in the vote that overrode Taft's veto, and the interstate measure became law.

Sawney himself introduced a bill to protect the flag, and prevailed on the Senate, but not the House, to pass it. He was incensed to find the Stars and Stripes on packages of tobacco. His measure mainly struck at commercial prostitution of the flag. A concluding section, nevertheless, covered malicious destruction. He hated to see the American symbol cheapened. The old man was a completely reconstructed Rebel.

One Sunday he went to see his old boy Clovis Chappell, now the pastor of Mount Vernon Methodist Church. He chatted with the young minister in his study. During the sermon, he sat in the congregation, listening with the devotion Clovis's own father would have given. Toward the end, the preacher began paying him a tribute, and the old man broke down and wept with his face in his hands. An old lady behind him bent over and asked: "Don't you think it's time you surrendered to the Lord?"

"I've been a Christian all my life," Old Sawney replied. "But how did you like the minister? . . . I raised him."

He was invited to the inauguration of President Wilson. His old boy William McCombs had managed Wilson's campaign. Now

McCombs was Democratic national chairman. But Sawney remembered William as a frail little fellow with one leg inches shorter than the other. How strange, the eternal possibilities of a boy. . . . Senator Webb was naturally a Wilson man. Years before, he had looked on the Princeton teacher as a statesman. Now as the president-elect delivered his address, the village schoolmaster stood near him on the left. When the *Literary Digest* reported the inauguration, Sawney's own face, with windswept hair and snowy beard, was in the cover picture.

It had been a most improbable journey from a moldy church basement. Sawney Webb was the "Grand Old Man of Tennessee." After his return from Washington, there was talk of his running for governor. He declared that the excitement of a hotly fought campaign would kill him. It was excitement enough during these years to be reading about all of the "old boys" that he and John had taught: the new U.S. Attorney General Watt Gregory, for example, a fatherless youth, whose widowed mother had run a boarding house at Culleoka. There had seemed to be a question in the boy's strong mind whether Watt, or he, Sawney Webb, should run the school. Sawney chuckled. . . .

Another "old boy," U.S. Undersecretary of State Norman Davis, later president of the American Red Cross, was proud of a conversation he had with Wilson. Davis and the president were discussing classical learning, en route home aboard a liner from the Peace Conference. Davis was reminiscing on his old school's classical emphasis. Wilson asked him what the name of that school might be. Though Davis doubted very much that the president had ever heard of it, he told Wilson it was Webb, in Bell Buckle, Tennessee. "Much to my delight," Norman Davis reported, "he said in substance: 'I not only know about that school but when I was president of Princeton, I considered it about the best preparatory school in the country. I thought so highly of it that I went down there once and spent a week with Sawney and Johnnie Webb, who were two most remarkable men, and so very different.' " This "old boy's" father was a distiller. Sending Norman and other sons to Webb had surprised Old Sawney. But according to a Webb family story, Ky Davis told the schoolmaster they agreed on educating boys, regardless of Mr. Webb's Prohibition politics.

Another old boy, a college president, became U.S. commissioner of education. John Tigert was one of eight Webb School Rhodes scholars—the largest number then from any one secondary school. Old Johnny had awakened Tigert's love of good reading, and had helped guide him toward his distinguished career. In his later years, Tigert also paid tribute to Old Sawney, for his "uncanny insight into the nature of boys" in originating a school that "in some respects . . . long ante-dated modern schools. . . ."

Neither Sawney nor John is likely to have known that two graduates held the one-time best entrance records at Harvard. Not too many years after World War I, young Professor William Y. Elliott asked the chairman of admissions who had been the best-prepared freshman of Harvard College. The official replied that the highest entrance tests were written by two boys from a school in Tennessee Elliott probably never heard of—but Rhodes Scholar Elliott's own association with Webb was the very reason he had asked his question. "Old boy" Elliott knew the school from the inside, as did his father, three Princeton uncles, and his brother.

Many old boys had gone out to teach throughout the South and all over Tennessee. A number had established other schools of quality: Morgan (as early as the Culleoka days), Branham & Hughes, Fitzgerald & Clarke, Massey, Peoples-Tucker, Duncan, Price-Webb, Battleground Academy—these and others thrived on a recognized model of excellence. They never became me-too's in policy or personality.

This independent growth of family-type schools was unique in the South—and probably in nineteenth-century America. Their pluralism was of promising human benefit, for if a student did not thrive in one, he might respond successfully in another. Webb and Branham & Hughes actually practiced exchanging boys, to the benefit of everyone concerned. Big trends in education, however, were look-alike, impersonal, mechanical, and monolithic. They bothered Old Sawney as much as they were troubling Old Johnny. The well-clocked Carnegie unit of education was becoming the national norm. Men were letting machines take over the judgment of learning. Webb's best prepared boys had to take entrance tests at Vanderbilt, while students with the "hours-guarantee" gained direct admission. Old Johnny's son Professor Albert Webb remembered a young woman graduate of Bell Buckle who, though valedictorian of her Vanderbilt class, never had her admissions credits accepted.

Old Sawney repeatedly deplored the trend toward giant schools on the secondary level: "The greatest value of my schooldays from the beginning to graduation was the inspiration that came from contact with great personalities that were made possible by small bodies of students. . . . The inspiration is the essential and only essential." The inspiration. After all, the two greatest and most effective teachers of the western world were not too proud to work with only a relatively few students at a time. But Socrates and Jesus were beside the point to the Southern Association of Colleges and Schools. The association's oldest and most celebrated secondary-school member was stubbornly refusing to play the academic game.

Yet the SACS leadership could bide their time. The irascible old man of Bell Buckle could not last forever, and besides the school was decidedly out of date. So SACS continued to print their list of secondary-school members, and table their "approved" schools separately. Both lists were becoming endless, anyway. SACS did not drop rebellious Webb School until immediately after the death of Sawney Webb. Only then did they combine the two lists of schools, omitting Webb, and make complicated tables of them in a book-length appendix. It was impersonally done, and years later, Son Will regained the approval of the association. But the best in the human spirit was finding it uncommonly hard to survive the mechanics of so-called education.

Toward the close of John Webb's life and career, some of his Bell Buckle students even organized a "union," which put social pressures on any boy who dared do more than a standard minimum. For years most of Old Jack's boys had responded heartily to his challenges, but he sorrowfully told his son that he found it impossible to break down the "union" barrier.

In the winter of 1916, Rhodes Scholar John Andrew Rice, who had returned to Webb to teach, found his beloved teacher incoherent and stumbling along Bell Buckle's railroad tracks. John was suffering a severe stroke. The trouble between the two principals' families reached a climax. Albert began to talk with Old Sawney about the interest in the school to which his stricken father was entitled.

"I never heard it alluded to before," Sawney told his lawyer son Clary. "Oh! how I would grieve to have our affairs aired before the public. I educated my brother when it took all the money and all I could borrow. I made sacrifices for him. I have relieved him of all drudgery in school work, the lower classes, the discipline and book-keeping and the unpleasant interviews, the boarding house con-

troversies. I traveled with him again and again, when he was helpless in mind. I have loved him all my life. I do not wish Albert to
stir up any controversies about business affairs." The unwished
controversy did occur. Lack of a definite previous understanding
made it worse.

On April 5, 1916, John Webb died. He was buried in an un-
marked grave in Hazelwood Cemetery on the hill, near his infant
son who gave the cemetery its name. The South's intellectual leadership was represented at his quiet funeral. Many an old boy gave
his deepest thanks for John Webb's life. Far more than a remarkable scholar and magnificent teacher, he had been a wise and un-
assuming lifetime friend. He had also blessed the year of many a
youth's most painful uncertainty.

Partnerships dissolve at death. Estrangement with John's family
was an obvious fact. Sawney mailed Lily a letter of condolence and
a check, reputably for $5,000. He undoubtedly believed his gesture
to be not ungenerous. To Lily Shipp Webb, it was far worse than
ungenerous. She wrote an impassioned demand for "justice." She
was certain that her brother-in-law had scarcely any notion of the
precious achievements and accomplishments of her husband. Moreover, long after Sawney retired from the classroom, and while Sawney went on speaking tours and even pranced off to Washington,
dear John continued to carry his classroom load.

She thought Albert had as much right to succeed his father as
Son Will had to be a principal already. Daughter Mary's husband
Stewart Mims intensely desired to join Albert in guiding the school.
Stewart was a most capable "old boy." They knew Will had been
unpopular with many boys since the year he returned and replaced
his father in the classroom. Some dissidents thought he was harder
on students than his father. Albert threatened to take the case to
federal court.

An "old boy" from Memphis represented the John Webb family. He was Walter Armstrong, later president of the American Bar
Association. Son Clary represented Sawney and settlement came
quickly. A court case was publicity they could do without. The figure awarded to John Webb's family is believed to have been about
$15,000. Years later, another alumnus attorney quoted Armstrong
as saying the settlement was fair.

Immediately afterward, the John Webb family abandoned Bell
Buckle. They sold the home and other properties quickly. The

gentle scholar was gone. The school-and-family rupture was complete. Ever since, some partisans have accused Old Sawney of taking the school away from his younger brother.

However, the one outside participant in the case never believed that Old Sawney was morally reprehensible. He had been in a position to hear the worst that Lily Webb could say in her grief and bitterness. Yet he invariably talked to his own family of Old Sawney in terms of the deepest respect. At the urging of friends and scholars, he even considered writing the schoolmaker's biography, and he paid oral and written tribute to his "humanity." According to his own son, attorney Walter Armstrong "continued to feel that way to the end."

The family misunderstanding went far beyond money. It went to the heart of the family problem of fatherhood. It went to the heart of the human problem of government. No man or woman in authority can avoid harsh criticism and bitter enmity—excesses of healthy human reservations about established power. Others may seek to save in an advisory capacity, but the responsible leader carries the risks of progress. He can also count on a human desire to believe the worst of him. It was rumored that this famous Sawney Webb, who allowed no gambling among his schoolboys, had lost his own life savings in the nineties, betting on one of Little Brown Jug's fast-pacing kinfolks. It was believed that the school was a gold mine and that Sawney was making big money as an educator. Yet he kept tuition low in spite of inflation, he persisted in giving scholarships to deserving students, and he provoked the charge he was taking unfair advantage of his neighbors by insisting that landladies hold their own rates in line.

He flatly refused to reply publicly to attacks made on his character. His resolute silence was distressing to his children, but he would not for all the world become an explainer. It was nobody else's business that his conservative speculation in land had been successful or that his own thrift had made it possible. He pinched pennies on principle. On a train trip, he was forever carrying one of Emma's sack lunches along. He would not enter a railroad diner, with its outrageous prices.

Now that he had survived and prevailed and won his wars, the Grand Old Man became a public symbol, for a season enjoying the allegiance of most segments of the patched but unhealed southern society. Editorial writers almost apologized when they found it necessary to disagree with him. Admirers seemed to invest him with perfection and infallibility. For many he became more than the ideal southern schoolmaster. He even stood for the grandeur of the romantic southern past, the incarnation of southern white supremacy. He had reached that level of publicity where the popular mind treats a man as a god—or as a devil. It would become easy, sooner or later, for enemies to turn his very virtues into vices. The glory years of the school grew into a grim decade of coming to terms in the wider society with some frightful human failures. The old survivor of war, famine, panic, plague, and social revolution still held on tight to his faith in progress. Yet as a veteran handler of hatred and resentment, he had often pondered the tragic meanings in evolution.

"I sometimes wonder," he told students, "how it is possible on any other line to account for the fact that we don't live together in peace, that we don't live together just because we love each other. . . . A man walks up to me and tells me I'm a liar . . . I draw back to hit him . . . knock his face around. . . . I see him swallowing his bloody teeth. Does that prove that I am not a liar? There isn't any genius on the earth that can explain it: I see two dogs jump on one another. . . . I see two strange hens. They begin to ruffle their feathers. And Darwinism, I think sometimes, is true and we have inherited these things. My resentment don't prove anything on the face of the earth except my kinship to lower animal life."

Sawney had also watched members of two races "jump on one another" in a variety of historical circumstances. Now the protracted epidemic of lynchings, particularly in the South, was culminating in outbreaks of racial violence, South and North. As a responsible school authority, he had always been caught between his sense of justice and the practical necessity of living by the unequal laws of the patched but unhealed southern society. "Race prejudice is a fact. It is wrong. . . . You are going to have nothing to do with any Negro," he told his students. The application of this school rule was not one-sided with him. He was moved to indignation by a student's attempt to take advantage of the inequality.

"Now a case came up last Friday," he told his students one morning in 1902. "A boy met a colored girl in a secluded spot by a creek. He asked her if she didn't want a piece of money. She resented it. I asked him if he had ever been introduced to her. He said, 'No.' Then I said, 'You had no right to speak to her.' You say, 'Mr. Webb, do you draw these lines so closely as that?' 'Yes.' The fellow that isn't as polite to a colored girl as to a queen, he isn't a gentleman. When the boy asked her the question, 'Do you want a piece of money?' she resented it with a vile term, as the boy says. Then he drew his knife and rushed at her and told her to take it back. I told him he could go home at once.

"I feel sorry for a poor man. He can't have good clothes, nor good food, nor many of the ordinary comforts of life. He feels it. Oftentimes he won't take a meal with a friend nor go to church because his clothes are not good enough. When a little dude passes a man like that and feels above him, he is a contemptible thing in my sight. I feel sorry for the poor Negro. He is not my equal. He knows it. He has to do menial work all the time. I would like to treat him well. A Negro girl wants to better her lot. She gets a little better education than the rest of her race around her. She teaches a little country school and as she walks along the public highway she is insulted by a white boy. Reverse the scene. Let a Negro walk up to a white girl in a secluded spot and say, "Don't you want a piece of money?' I sometimes wish the Negroes would rise up and hang some of these miserable sneaks that insult their women. I don't believe the white men would do anything to them."

Sawney's insistence on justice and politeness was one thing. His personal belief and social attitude was another. Like a majority of white Americans then, he was convinced that Negroes in general were racially inferior. Yet his approach to the racial problem remained progressive. In his seventy-seventh year he went out of his way to make a special plea through his church for better interracial communication. As social service chairman, he sought adoption of a report calling for "national, state and neighborhood conferences of leaders from both races," with a frank interchange of opinions concerning "traveling, housing, educational, moral and religious conditions," followed by "an honest effort to understand the causes of bad feeling." It was 1919. The idea was behind its time—but, unfortunately, too far ahead of it as well. The fact that he made that special speech, and the wording of the social service report, remain a part of the Methodists' Tennessee Conference records.

The tragedy of World War I had also come. Old Sawney served on Bedford County's "draft exemption board" and grieved over decisions he sometimes had to make. He wrote a letter of encouragement to all his "old boys" in uniform. He tried to cheer up a group

of student teachers: "I do want to say to you that with all this tragedy of war going on here, we will yet find that the results of that
war are going to be beneficial to us in every respect. We were fast
becoming a nation given up to selfish indulgence, fast becoming so,
basing too much on the almighty dollar, and now we have got to
share it, and it is going to do us good. We are going to raise this $35
million in gifts for the YMCA, like we raised $100 million for the
Red Cross. It is splendid. . . ." He also welcomed the peace plans of
President Wilson.

Half a century before, the most tragic period of national history
had disciplined him to optimism as the best means to endure and
survive and prevail—that and the promise of an exhortation which
he credited with possibly having encouraged him more than any
other: "Let us not be weary in well-doing, for in due season we shall
reap if we faint not."

Oh yes! He knew he had made mistakes. He also knew he had not
fainted.

XVI. The Parting Vision:
Electricity...Electricity

Life is an opportunity.
It takes drilling from experience
that we may appreciate
that opportunity.
—SAWNEY WEBB

He did not go gentle....

"The grinders are low, the hearing is sluggish, and I don't think the *light* is as good as it used to be," he wrote a friend. His wide eyes of crockery blue were a little watery and withdrawn behind the windows of the spectacles he always wore. His voice was also growing high and thin. But the Grand Old Man refused to abandon his morning trip to the Big Room. Son Will was certain Father wanted—even expected—to die there.

As the two stood talking near the bookboard one morning, neither noticed that some student had placed an enormous horned owl on top of the Bible to see what the bouncy octogenarian would do. Son Thompson, who was teaching at Bell Buckle then, expected Father to do plenty, and so did many others watching. The bird was alive. As Old Sawney continued to talk to Will, he reached out toward the lectern without looking, and found his hand on the big owl's feathers. He stepped back instantly, and almost before his feet touched the floor, he said: "Boys, the Bird of Wisdom is in the right place this morning."

The Big Room shook with the spontaneous roar of laughter, recognition, and applause. As Old Sawney pushed the owl over, just off the Bible, most boys knew that Proverbs, the First Chapter, had to be coming: "The instruction of wisdom . . . my son," he read it again. *Get wisdom. Get understanding.* . . . He was never afraid to repeat a passage endlessly, until even the inattentive could not help learning. In his morning talk he described Minerva, the Roman Goddess of Wisdom, and he explained that she decreed the owl was sacred, and caused the bird to be identified with the wise.

He knew how to touch the spirits of young and old. He visited his antebellum teacher, Colonel Robert Bingham, and wrote him a letter of tribute afterwards: "You ought to be thankful that your mind is clear even though you have difficulty expressing it in a rickety machine. . . . I have met no one better posted on current events, and whose splendid philosophy adjusted him better to these latter days—notwithstanding in your life-time, there has been a complete revolution of man's life physically, intellectually, and religiously. You graciously and sensibly adjusted yourself to the wonderful changes that have come in your day."

On this old teacher's eighty-fifth birthday, Old Sawney addressed a Bingham School reunion. Robert had taken over at Mebane when William died, and moved the school west again—at last to the mountain city of Asheville. He had been kind there to Sawney's daughter Emma. She was caring for an infant daughter and nursing her dying husband. Dr. Dugald McLean was another of Bell Buckle's Rhodes scholars. The young physician wrote a treatise on his own case of tuberculosis, finishing it just before his death.

Emma with the moist blue eyes, the gentlest of his eight children, was to become a young widow, like his mother. He wrote her: "You have developed into a noble woman and I am proud of you. . . . 'Verily Thou art a God that hidest Thyself' is a text that has come to me many a time in this mysterious chain of life. Life is an opportunity. It takes drilling from experience that we may appreciate that opportunity."

He was thankful he had spent his own life "worrying with boys." It was almost sixty years now and he had not missed a term. "I have been in the best company this side of heaven . . . the boy may be careless, thoughtless, or mischievous, but he is seldom bad." He was asked what he would do differently if he could live his life over. "I'd play more," Old Sawney promptly replied.

On an early anniversary of the armistice, he arrived at a college town in Georgia. A brass band was playing. Festive displays of bunting and the flag decorated the streets. He attracted the attention of three male students as he emerged from the train in his rumpled suit, misbuttoned vest, and the inevitably misplaced string tie, which he said had gone in and out of style three times. He read their merry young thoughts and asked with great seriousness how the town knew it was his birthday, as in truth, it was. The three students, wearing straight faces, instructed the white-bearded hillbilly that this was a celebration of the end of the recent war. That night, their hillbilly was a featured speaker. He spotted his three victims in the front row, pointed his finger in their direction, and addressed his entire speech at the abashed young men.

Sawney's neckpiece was so famous that a boy won the Liars Club championship at Vanderbilt with the statement he had once seen Old Sawney with his tie on straight. He was a walking legend, a talking museum piece, a publicity saint, a symbol of survive and prevail. He could say in the Big Room with some amusement, and maybe a little wonder: "You new boys, take a good look at me. I'm the old cuss you've heard so much about."

In 1920, the *Atlantic Monthly* published an article about "Old Sawney's." His own alma mater awarded him an honorary doctorate in 1922, for "establishing the first training school west of the Alleghenies." Erskine College had honored him in the same way. Three decades before, he had actually been elected to the Headmasters Association, one of the first two southern members of that New England collection of wise and venerable autocrats.

Citizens of Culleoka even invited the old warrior back to dedicate their new school building. Here he found the sweet taste of reconciliation. The daughter of his friend, the late Claiborne Taylor, told him that this was the greatest compliment he could receive. Yet he was facing the realities of his age. "I am a back number," he told young student teachers at Peabody College. He knew he was out of style. His one-man platform approach could not survive the proliferation of new media, the excitement of photographs in magazines and newspapers, the coming of radio, the mobile distractions of the motor car, the glowing kaleidoscope of instant pleasures in the growing electrical cities. The crowds went along with the current.

Technology was giving man so many new angles that man figured he could now dispense with old-fashioned virtues. Psychologists were using apes and infants to prove that the will did not exist—so why try to "educate" it? Strict morality was distinctly unfashionable. It had already gone too far, many people agreed. Prohibition was proving to be so ghastly that Old Sawney himself told his son Thompson it had been a fatal mistake not to leave both beer and wine legal. What idealists achieve does not always turn into Progress. The twenties roared.

Change was deeply affecting the Bell Buckle school. The old boarding house system was doomed. Wartime inflation had pushed food prices out of sight. Good Negro cooks disappeared in the great migration North and East. As war had ended Old Bingham's boarding house system, so the effects of war were ending the system at Old Sawney's. A new generation of parents were insisting on more creature comforts. Cornshuck mattresses and freezing baths in galvanized tubs deserved to remain in the nineteenth century.

Devoted alumni begged Old Sawney to let them build a dormitory. But more "immovable real estate" was what he preferred most to avoid. At last Son Will successfully prevailed on his father and Webb–Bell Buckle entered its red-brick era. A group of alumni incorporated the "Board of Trustees of Webb School" in order to conserve the property. The old stock company was moribund. Up went two sprawling unpretentious structures, trimmed with white-painted wooden pediments and gables. Jackson Dormitory, in 1921, and Rand Dormitory, in 1925, were named for very generous old boys.

More than mere physical changes were ahead. Curriculum would change. The natural sciences would come. Sawney had abandoned them at Culleoka as a sham—as indeed they were. He knew science required laboratories that the school could not then afford. He believed that thoroughness in a few subjects was more valuable than a smattering of many. He did see to it that boys mastered the language of science, basic mathematics. He did not believe that boy or man should try to spread himself over the whole earth. Although the sciences must come, Webb–Bell Buckle would adhere to thorough mastery.

Boy-girl relations were changing, too. Although he seemed backwardly Victorian, Old Sawney felt he had been Progressive. "It would have been absolutely barbarous in my day," he said, "for girls to come to Bingham School, or to the University of North

Carolina. . . . A wonderful revolution! I don't think the revolution could have occurred unless boys and girls got better than they were." In Culleoka he started out by letting the boys call on the girls. However, as the school grew larger, he felt there were not enough girls "of the right type." He did not dare discriminate among fathers' daughters in a very small town. "So I had to draw a line on the whole thing." Boys could go with girls only during Commencement Week, and only to and from Big Room performances, without stopping. If a passing freight train caught a boy escorting a girl home, he would blithely walk around her in circles, keeping the rule, until the long train had finally passed. As one old boy put it, girls were generally to be looked at but not talked to: "There was no sitting in the swing, no parlor talk, no romancing. Yet how precious this forbidden fruit was made to seem. Looking back on it, I can think of several esteemed fellows of mine who have been making up ever since for those lost opportunities."

Although many people thought he was rigid, Sawney never opposed doing things differently. He did not admire "the lots of people who do not want any change." He did not even think that children should copy their parents. Now Thompson was a struggling schoolmaker out West, and Sawney poured out his experience in passionate letters of advice to his youngest son. In the early twenties, he saw room for considerable change on the educational scene. "A child ought to love to go to school," he said. "I believe that one of the greatest cases against our people of the United States is that they put good, straight children in jail all day long." He emphasized principles of wise flexibility: "You must be yourself. You cannot be anybody else, however much you try. . . . You cannot have the discipline and habits of Webb School at the start. I started without any trained boys to lead. . . . It took one or two years before I dared to have a pledge based on [a boy's] word of honor as a gentleman. You will have to adapt yourself and your school to conditions of environment as shown in public sentiment. . . . You can gradually elevate that sentiment in school and out. . . . Make rules gradually. . . . Stress character above everything—scholarship *too* above sports. Let sports be a re-creation after real work. That is its function. . . . You will have to watch every dime. . . . Keep an account of every cent and you can often see a way to save expenses."

In 1923, Sawney and Emma went to see their son. They traveled by train to southern California. They found Thompson on a dry adobe hillside near Claremont, with his pretty wife Vivian, and their own family of sons. They also saw the new Webb School of California, in old frame buildings among yucca and a few palms. Then Thompson made a trembling confession. He told of his nip-and-tuck "wildcat financing." Sawney surprised his son by roaring with laughter. It sounded so much like his own early troubles. But he cautioned Thompson to keep paying his interest on time.

Sawney was glad Thompson's school was near Pomona College. He attended a symposium on education on the campus in Claremont. A speaker was praising the virtues of "manual training." Old Sawney approved, though he preferred the simpler term "hand work." But then the speaker began to disparage Latin and said he would much rather have his sons learn to milk a cow. After the speech Old Sawney asked for the floor, and told the audience that he thoroughly approved practical skills. He was so happy to have raised his own four sons on a farm and taught them all how to milk. He concluded, however, that so far as the speaker's attitude toward Latin was concerned, "I want my son to know how to do something that a calf can't beat him at." The wit and laughter echoed all the way into New England.

At home in Bell Buckle in April of 1923, he and Emma celebrated their golden wedding anniversary. Hundreds paid calls. Telegrams and cards poured in. Sawney paid tribute to the "model woman" his wife was, and wondered at her, still without a gray hair, and still with natural color in her cheeks. Emma's paintings of country landscapes hung on the walls of their home.

On Sunday morning, he continued to take his place in Amen Corner, in a pew at the left ear of the preacher. Spectators watched him wag one foot when he crossed his knees, and fearfully invested it with special meanings. The preacher was sure that when the foot speeded up, Old Sawney was disagreeing with the sermon. The boys watched it for fear it would stop, for then they were sure he knew they were not paying attention.

People in the country still called on him to speak to them and he continued to travel the difficult, dusty roads. He had managed to acquire the skill of driving a car, but it lacked the sense of a horse. Sawney could not muse while he drove it. Many villagers distrusted him at the wheel. At least once he ran the contraption off the road, into a farmer's field. Webb Follin, an old boy, teacher, and later Bell Buckle's principal, often traveled with the old man on his trips. Before twin beds came into small-town hotels, he recalled, "It was like climbing into bed with Moses."

In 1924, Sawney drove his own automobile over the mountains, in the company of his wife and his daughter Alla. He spoke out in a news interview against the Klan. He deplored the religious bigotry that characterized its recent revival, and cited the Catholic chaplain who had ministered to him on the slopes of Malvern Hill. He visited Tip in North Carolina on his brother's own sixtieth wedding anniversary. Sawney also attended the special session of the Methodist General Conference, which voted reunion with the northern church. He was proud to be the oldest delegate in 1924, as he had been the youngest years before.

The next year he was thrilled by the round-the-world flight of four Army Air Corps fliers. His "old boy" Lieutenant Jack Harding was one of them, and en route mailed a card, which went something like this: "Mr. Webb, I'm not driving a quarter horse. I've got one that takes the same gait all the time." His "boys" often sent him messages, repeating his famous sayings. Some wrote him postcards from Colorado, recalling his lecture on "Pike's Peak or Bust!"

In 1925 the famous Scopes "Monkey" Trial got under way. Dayton was only about seventy-five miles to the east. The old man had pondered evolution for most of his life. Now he began reading all the books he could find on the subject. Afterwards, he told his youngest son that though it went against his earlier beliefs, he concluded those scientists had just about proved their theory. Yet he was never more firm in his religious faith, and continued trying to deepen his understanding. In his last conversation with one old boy, he said: "I'm trying to learn all I can about the Holy Ghost."

In November of 1925, his wife broke her hip. She was confined to her room in virtual helplessness for many months. He was terribly lonely. He lived very much alone. Because of his deafness he avoided gatherings, even in his home. "I feel like a nuisance," he confided to a friend. He also felt it very keenly that younger friends did not come to visit him. He had told his boys for a lifetime not to loaf in the village. So he sat by himself in his office at home, and listened to the trains passing. The "light" was dimmer. He could hardly read.

That summer of 1926 he was unusually slow in recovering from a minor illness. By October his condition was serious. A second Dr. Freeman doubted Sawney could get well, with his leaky heart valve.

In November he grew worse, with pneumonia. In his rational moments, he begged Son Will to put Webb School ahead of him. He worried lest the boys be depressed by his illness. Will must not neglect school correspondence. And if he should beg for Will in a delirium, Will must ignore him, if coming meant Will had to neglect the boys.

He was restless and in pain. There were a number of uncomfortable, sleepless nights. But narcotics made him wild and uncontrollable. He raged and thrashed around in a panic of delirious anxiety. They tried bromide, and it worked. At last he slept very well on the night of Friday, December 17. As Will arrived the next morning, he and his sisters heard Father screaming. It was one of the weirdest sounds he had ever heard. The emaciated old man was straining to get up. His beard shook. He was terribly excited. At last, they understood: their dying father was searching for adequate words. He knew he was at the very Gates of Heaven.

Old Sawney said he saw all of his lost loved ones again. His mother, Sister Suny, his brother-in-law Dr. Will Clary. Dear friends like old Dr. Freeman. "Iron Duke" Methodist Tillett. Dozens more. He saw Dugald, his "old boy," his dead son-in-law, Emma's husband. His own mother was young again and beautiful. He turned to his wife and said that "over there" they would be bride and groom again, and never grow old. There were thousands and thousands in the heavenly crowd. He knew them every one. He could call the roll.

Then all at once the old man grew deeply disturbed. Sawney could not find his father anywhere. Where was his father? He wanted his father! It took Sister Suny to quiet him in his vision. She explained that their father had died when he was too young to remember him. She pointed him out—the Man with the Basket of Corn—and Sawney gave a shout of relief and joy. In these hours, and days, he frequently said softly: "I am so glad . . . I am so glad."

Then Old Sawney saw John again. His younger brother was living in a beautiful house. He was standing with his son, a most handsome young man, a great artist who had decorated their home. Brother Sawney was overjoyed. It was Hazel, their dead cousin, the children thought. Then Sawney described a little girl of six. She must be brother Thompson's daughter, who had died. Old Sawney declared that he could even see into his boyhood. "Electricity . . . electricity . . . electricity !" he kept shouting. The children assumed their father meant the heavenly light. But "Electricity" was the name for something in his life. Was he thinking of that beloved mare who took a fatal bullet intended for him in the last days of the Civil War, the war horse who had been shot out from under him?

He continued straining to get up. Dr. Freeman warned Will not to hold him. If he exerted any physical effort, his heart would stop. Finally Sawney exclaimed that now he saw William Bingham, his brilliant old teacher. "Yes, Father, you see him, and listen: he wants you to lie down and rest." Father promptly sank back upon the pillow, and said, "I never disobeyed him in my life." Gradually, he dropped off to sleep. This time he never noticed the hypodermic. On Sunday, December 19, he barely awakened, but in an effort to turn over, at 7:45 a.m. his heart grew still. The 84-year-old body had simply worn out.

Two Nashville radio stations announced the news. On Monday there were obituaries in newspapers across the country. Telegrams of condolence, followed by hundreds of letters, poured into the village from everywhere. They seemed to prove, as Old Sawney had said, "The sun never sets on a Webb School boy." That afternoon the Dixie Flyer made a special stop in the village in time to bring out-of-town friends to the funeral. The school faculty, as pallbearers, arrived at Sawney House. They included Assistant Principal Follin and former teacher John Clary, a son of the late Dr. Clary. They carried the casket out of the old man's booklined office, and down the damp front steps between the Ionic pillars. They were wearing raincoats. A cold, heavy rain was pouring down. The ivy-covered red-brick church with the tower was just half a wet block south, down Maple. The pallbearers carried the casket along the sidewalk, strewn with the fallen leaves from trees that Emma and Sawney had planted. Hundreds of mourners with dripping umbrellas crowded the sanctuary. The platform was banked with flowers.

One of Old Sawney's first students opened the brief service. He was Dr. W. F. Tillett, the "Iron Duke's" son, now dean of the theology department at Vanderbilt. This was the onetime stammering youth at Horner's, whom a young Sawney had taught how to "learn one thing at a time." Dr. Tillett explained the funeral was simple at the request of his old teacher "whom we long ago learned to obey and whose body is there embedded in flowers." Then he proceeded with the Methodist burial ritual.

A small choir sang "It Is Well with My Soul." There was also a prayer. A score of Webb students attended although school had been dismissed for Christmas. They helped load the seventy-five floral displays on trucks for the trip to Hazelwood Cemetery. The December rain continued to flood the land. The hundred-car procession drove down Maple to Main and over the tracks, south again on a road past the vacant brick saloon, then a westward winding up the hill to the cemetery. A tent and a waterproof metal vault protected Old Sawney's grave. Surrounded by the soaked red soil, he was laid to rest at last.

Newspapers were full of reminiscences. Memorial services took place in Nashville and in other communities. Published eulogies to the "South's greatest teacher of boys" were endless. There were also unusual echoes of his passing.

Son John in California dreamed of a great host surrounding his father. When John reached him, with difficulty, he asked Father who they were. "Son," Old Sawney replied, "don't you know them? Here are Caesar, Cicero, Ovid, Virgil, and that's Homer over there." John was the only one of his sons who had resisted the classics.

The youngest son Thompson in California was in the midst of the struggle of his life. He was fighting to keep his new school going. The night after the sad news Thompson saw his father bending over him and saying: "Keep up the fight, son! Be not weary in well-doing. . . ." The Way never would be an easy one.

Back east in the Blue Ridge mountains, hikers found Webb Tower broken.

At home in Bell Buckle, his family opened his wallet and found dozens of characteristic items: a snapshot, pieces of poetry, receipts, little homilies on the importance of education, newspaper clippings. There was also an unidentified editorial tribute to the wit of that famous old boy Ned Carmack, that clever master of extemporaneous humor, "the most brilliant story teller that ever came to Washington."

On his deathbed Old Sawney had also dictated to Son Will one last message to all his living sons in the spirit: "Give my boys my love and tell them to lead a large life. A large life is no mere piffle but one that makes the world better because you have lived. If the world is better because of you, you are a wonderful success. If it's worse because of you, you are a miserable failure. When you come to the end, you will find that the only things that are worth while are character and the help you've given to other people. The first step in the development of character is loyalty and obedience to your parents, your teacher and to God. And don't forget, don't do anything that you've got to hide."

Epilogue

Character is an educated will.
—SAWNEY WEBB

Old Sawney's school survived. It became the seat of a tradition. Webb–Bell Buckle entered its second century of life in spite of conflict and adversity. Even old boys that resented the discipline could love the place and respect the man. John Andrew Rice, author of the unkindest words about him ever published, could pay this tribute to the school Old Sawney built and governed: "In later years, when I bore the dubious title of educator, and at last was tagged with the still more dubious 'Progressive,' I visited schools and listened to breathless accounts of the latest thing. I could match them point by point from the Webb School I knew as a student, and go them one better—two better, for the school had both order and intellectual backbone. As to the rest, its government was for boys as no school I have seen since."

It was the impetus of Old Sawney as a great motivator that kept the Bell Buckle School alive long after many of its brother and sister schools had perished in the wake of improved public schools, a more permissive educational philosophy, and galloping inflation, followed by the Great Depression. Old boys themselves continued to make distinctive contributions to education as well as to other professions. Sawney's own family continued to make schools in a struggling and somewhat risky way, and the way has spread.

Webb School of California, founded in 1922 by Old Sawney's

youngest son, is close to the celebration of its fiftieth anniversary, and like its parent school, has given impetus to the making of other schools. W. R. (Bob) Webb III, third generation namesake of Old Sawney, founded the Webb School of Knoxville in 1955. Another grandson that bears the earlier schoolmaker's name, W. R. (Bill) Webb IV, has become a headmaster in California, and still another grandson, Howell Webb, is founding headmaster of a primary day school in Claremont, California.

The founder of the second Webb School, Thompson Webb of Claremont, was instrumental during the 1930s in developing the concept of responsible "independence," in contrast to "privatism," in the non-public school movement of California. Later he took part in a corresponding movement throughout the nation, organized today as the National Association of Independent Schools, with headquarters in Boston. The Webb tradition is but one of many diverse elements in this pluralistic development of schools below the college level.

After Sawney's death, Webb–Bell Buckle heroically fought to remain alive in a region that suffered severely from poverty and low income as late as World War II. Old boys struggled to maintain the school as Old Sawney had made it. The trustees, Principal William R. Webb, Jr., and his successor Webb Follin kept tuition remarkably low. They continued the outdoor study halls and the Honor System. Old boys loved the place so much that some of them fought for it with a powerful intensity. Those who heartily disliked it while they were there looked back on Bell Buckle as the crucial experience of their lives. Out of tradition came self-renewal.

Like most of the world around it, the school has changed. Greek has disappeared from the curriculum. Latin long ago ceased to be supreme. Wooden walls have given way to brick. Discipline has become considerably less severe. Yet the school community has remained committed to the struggle to foster high ethical standards, and a responsible Gospel of Do is the ideal still. According to Webb tradition, it is more appropriate for a school to put challenging demands on its students than for students to put militant demands on a school. As the valedictorian of another Webb school expressed it in 1967, there is "an emphasis upon self-discipline and perseverance." On the other hand, the tradition offers "in the untamed unconsolidated beauty of the surroundings, an atmosphere in which the natural world of insight, experience and experiential learning comes alive, a sort of Walden, apart from the world of deadlines and hard work."

Even as Bell Buckle entered the era of widespread student unrest, some of its youthful voices called for rededication to its long-time traditions. As one young man wrote in the student magazine, *The Oracle*, four years before Webb–Bell Buckle's hundredth birthday: "The answer to the students' protests will never be to ease their responsibilities, to lighten their extracurricular burdens. The only answer is to retain the pressures of study and citizenship, to convince the students that the quality of their school, its publications, and its activities depends solely on the amount of work they are willing to contribute, work beyond the point of pleasure, work sustained only by a strong, striving will to grow, to improve, and to survive."

Even at a time when schools across the nation heard their student bodies clamoring for greater responsibilities, Bell Buckle was busy applying new ways of sharing such responsibilities in dormitory, dining hall, and classroom, as well as on the athletic field. And those students who met the challenges gained the rewards.

The government of the school was for students still.

Index

Oaks. N.C.
Tuesday May 21ˢᵗ 1867.

Tawny dear, brother of my heart,

Like good
brother James you are too much off a
sensitive plant, & the world don't appreciate
such plants except for their rarity—
curiosities! Of course, from yⁱ brief note,
in which you are rather obscure any how,
I don't know all yⁱ reasons for declining
the trip to commencement, but I would
n't give it up, if I understand the
thing correctly. Miss Kate said you had
engaged to take Miss Landis some time
ago, but that she had since decided not
to attend commencement. I don't know
why. Miss Kate thinks you are in love, &
gave me to understand you were quite a
favorite with all the ladies. I heard of a
letter she wrote home when I first got to